Learn C# in 7 days

Get up and running with C# 7 with async main, tuples, pattern matching, LINQ, regex, indexers, and more

Gaurav Aroraa

BIRMINGHAM - MUMBAI

Learn C# in 7 days

First published: October 2017

Production reference: 1041017

Published by Packt Publishing Ltd.
Livery Place
35 Livery Street
Birmingham
B3 2PB, UK.

ISBN 978-1-78728-704-4

www.packtpub.com

Credits

Author
Gaurav Aroraa

Reviewer
Shivprasad Koirala

Commissioning Editor
Aaron Lazar

Acquisition Editor
Denim Pinto

Content Development Editor
Vikas Tiwari

Technical Editor
Diwakar Shukla

Copy Editor
Muktikant Garimella

Project Coordinator
Ulhas Kambali

Proofreader
Safis Editing

Indexer
Tejal Daruwale Soni

Graphics
Tania Dutta

Production Coordinator
Nilesh Mohite

About the Author

Gaurav Aroraa has an M.Phil in computer science. He is a Microsoft MVP, certified as a scrum trainer/coach, XEN for ITIL-F, and APMG for PRINCE-F and PRINCE-P. Gaurav serves as a mentor at IndiaMentor and the webmaster of dotnetspider. He is also a contributor to TechNet Wiki and a cofounder of Innatus Curo Software LLC. In the 19+ years of his career, he has mentored thousands of students and industry professionals. You can reach Gaurav via his blog, LinkedIn, or Twitter (`@g_arora`).

I want to thank all who motivated me and allowed me to spend time on this book, time that I was supposed to spend with them. My first thank you is to my wife, Shuby Arora, for her support in all ways. Then, I would like to thank my little angel, Aarchi Arora. A great thanks to my parents whose blessings are always with me; this is because of them. I would like to thank the entire Packt team, especially Vikas Tiwari, Diwakar Shukla, and Denim Pinto for their overnight support. A great thank you to Shivprasad Koirala for his in-depth knowledge and his suggestions to improve various sections of the book.

About the Reviewer

Shivprasad Koirala is an X-Microsoft MVP, Microsoft trainer, and technical author. He has written more than 80 books, and some of his bestsellers include *.NET interview questions* and *SQL Server interview questions*. You can catch him mostly recording training videos at `http://www.questpond.com`.

www.PacktPub.com

For support files and downloads related to your book, please visit www.PacktPub.com. Did you know that Packt offers eBook versions of every book published, with PDF and ePub files available? You can upgrade to the eBook version at www.PacktPub.com and as a print book customer, you are entitled to a discount on the eBook copy. Get in touch with us at service@packtpub.com for more details. At www.PacktPub.com, you can also read a collection of free technical articles, sign up for a range of free newsletters and receive exclusive discounts and offers on Packt books and eBooks.

https://www.packtpub.com/mapt

Get the most in-demand software skills with Mapt. Mapt gives you full access to all Packt books and video courses, as well as industry-leading tools to help you plan your personal development and advance your career.

Why subscribe?

- Fully searchable across every book published by Packt
- Copy and paste, print, and bookmark content
- On demand and accessible via a web browser

Customer Feedback

Thanks for purchasing this Packt book. At Packt, quality is at the heart of our editorial process. To help us improve, please leave us an honest review on this book's Amazon page at "Amazon Book URL". If you'd like to join our team of regular reviewers, you can email us at customerreviews@packtpub.com. We award our regular reviewers with free eBooks and videos in exchange for their valuable feedback. Help us be relentless in improving our products!

Table of Contents

Preface

Learning a new language or switching to an entirely different technology is a common industry demand. As a student one should prepare oneself to be up to date with market trends, and as a professional, one should be aware of the new things that are coming in with new technologies. To meet this demand, there are a lot of books that are of thousand pages long and aim to be comprehensive references to the C# programming language.

This book is entirely different and written so that someone who has a very basic knowledge of the C# language, or is a professional and working with another language but wants to switch, can learn C#. This book was designed with the aim that one should start with the basics and progress to an advanced level. The book contains concise content with relevant examples to explain everything.

There are a lot of sections in the book that will encourage you to learn more ; with this knowledge, you can impress your colleagues, employers, or batch-mates. There will be a few terms you will hear first time – no problem, you can learn about them in this book.

At the end of every section you will find a hands-on exercise section that will build confidence and give you ideas for solving practical problems. You can find various hints in these exercises.

For the code examples, you can go to the GitHub repository (`https://github.com/PacktPublishing/Learn-CSharp-in-7-days/`) and download the source code for all chapters. You can easily use these code example in Visual Studio 2017 Update 3 by following the instructions mentioned thereon.

What this book covers

`Chapter 1`, *Day 01 - Overview of the .NET Framework*, gets you familiar with C#, including .NET Framework and .NET Core.

`Chapter 2`, *Day 02 - Getting Started with C#*, gives you a basic understanding of C# by iterating through the type system and the use of various constructs. The use and importance of reserved keywords, understanding statements, type conversions.

`Chapter 3`, *Day 03 - What's New in C#*, gets you familiar with various new important features introduced in versions 7.0 and 7.1.

`Chapter 4`, *Day 04 - Discussing C# Class Members*, explains the fundamentals of class and its members will be explained including indexers, the filesystem, exception handling, and string manipulation with regular expressions.

Chapter 5, *Day 05 - Overview of Reflection and Collections*, covers working with code using reflection, and an introduction to collections, delegates, and events.

Chapter 6, *Day 06 - Deep Dive with Advanced Concepts,* teaches you about implementing attributes, using preprocessors, and understanding generics and their usage, including sync and async programming.

Chapter 7, *Day 07 - Understanding Object-Oriented Programming with C#,* In this chapter we will learn all 4-paradigm of oop and implement using C# 7.0.

Chapter 8, *Day 08 - Test Your Skills – Build a Real-World Application*, helps you to write a complete application with the help of what you learned from this book.

What you need for this book

All supporting code samples in this book have been tested on .NET Core 2.0 using Visual Studio 2017 update 3, database using SQL Server 2008R2 or later on the Windows platform.

Who this book is for

Learn C# in 7 Days is a fast-paced guide. In this book, we take a unique approach to teaching C# to an absolute beginner, who will be able to learn the basics of the language in seven days. This practical book comes with important concepts that introduce the foundation of the C# programming language. This book addresses the challenges and issues that most beginners face. It covers issues such as the need to learn C#, issues with setting up a development environment with C#, challenges such as mathematical operations, and other day-to-day problems. Its fast-paced writing style allows the reader to get up and running in no time. We begin with the absolute basics in the first chapter (variables, syntax, control flows, and so on), and then move on to concepts such as statements, arrays, string processing, methods, inheritance, I/O handling, and so on. Every chapter is followed by an exercise that focuses on building something with the language. This book is a fast-paced guide to get readers upto speed with the language. It works as a reference guide, describing the major features of C#. Readers will be able to build easy and simple code with real-world scenarios. By the end of this book, you will be able to take your skills to the next level, with a good knowledge of the fundamentals of C#.

Conventions

In this book, you will find a number of text styles that distinguish between different kinds of information. Here are some examples of these styles and an explanation of their meaning. Code words in text, database table names, folder names, filenames, file extensions, pathnames, dummy URLs, user input, and Twitter handles are shown as follows: "You will get the following code in the `Program.cs` class. This is the default code provided by Visual Studio; you can amend it as you need." A block of code is set as follows:

```
var class1 = newClassExample();
var class2 = new Day02New.ClassExample();
    class1.Display();
    class2.Display();
```

New terms and **important words** are shown in bold. Words that you see on the screen, for example, in menus or dialog boxes, appear in the text like this: "From **Workloads**, select the options you want to install. For our book, we need **.NET desktop development** and **.NET Core**."

Warnings or important notes appear like this.

Tips and tricks appear like this.

Reader feedback

Feedback from our readers is always welcome. Let us know what you think about this book-what you liked or disliked. Reader feedback is important for us as it helps us develop titles that you will really get the most out of. To send us general feedback, simply email feedback@packtpub.com, and mention the book's title in the subject of your message. If there is a topic that you have expertise in and you are interested in either writing or contributing to a book, see our author guide at www.packtpub.com/authors.

Customer support

Now that you are the proud owner of a Packt book, we have a number of things to help you to get the most from your purchase.

Downloading the example code

You can download the example code files for this book from your account at http://www.packtpub.com. If you purchased this book elsewhere, you can visit http://www.packtpub.com/support and register to have the files emailed directly to you. You can download the code files by following these steps:

1. Log in or register to our website using your email address and password.
2. Hover the mouse pointer on the **SUPPORT** tab at the top.
3. Click on **Code Downloads & Errata**.
4. Enter the name of the book in the **Search** box.
5. Select the book for which you're looking to download the code files.
6. Choose from the drop-down menu where you purchased this book from.
7. Click on **Code Download**.

Once the file is downloaded, please make sure that you unzip or extract the folder using the latest version of:

- WinRAR / 7-Zip for Windows
- Zipeg / iZip / UnRarX for Mac
- 7-Zip / PeaZip for Linux

The code bundle for the book is also hosted on GitHub at https://github.com/PacktPublishing/Learn-CSharp-in-7-Days. We also have other code bundles from our rich catalog of books and videos available at https://github.com/PacktPublishing/. Check them out!

Errata

Although we have taken every care to ensure the accuracy of our content, mistakes do happen. If you find a mistake in one of our books-maybe a mistake in the text or the code-we would be grateful if you could report this to us. By doing so, you can save other readers from frustration and help us improve subsequent versions of this book. If you find any errata, please report them by visiting http://www.packtpub.com/submit-errata, selecting your book, clicking on the **Errata Submission Form** link, and entering the details of your errata. Once your errata are verified, your submission will be accepted and the errata will be uploaded to our website or added to any list of existing errata under the Errata section of that title. To view the previously submitted errata, go to https://www.packtpub.com/books/content/support and enter the name of the book in the search field. The required information will appear under the **Errata** section.

Piracy

Piracy of copyrighted material on the internet is an ongoing problem across all media. At Packt, we take the protection of our copyright and licenses very seriously. If you come across any illegal copies of our works in any form on the internet, please provide us with the location address or website name immediately so that we can pursue a remedy. Please contact us at copyright@packtpub.com with a link to the suspected pirated material. We appreciate your help in protecting our authors and our ability to bring you valuable content.

Questions

If you have a problem with any aspect of this book, you can contact us at questions@packtpub.com, and we will do our best to address the problem.

1
Day 01 - Overview of the .NET Framework

This is Day 01 of our seven day journey to learn C#. Today, we will begin with an introduction of a new world of programming and will discuss all the basic concepts required to learn this programming language. We will also discuss the .NET Framework and the .NET Core framework by covering important concepts of the framework. We will also get a basic understanding of managed and unmanaged code. At the end of the day, we will start with a simple Hello World program.

Today, we will learn the following topics:

- What is programming?
- What is .NET Core?
- What is .NET standard?

What is programming?

There might be various definitions or various thoughts to define the word *programming*. In my view, *programming is writing a solution in such a way that a machine (computer) can understand to depict the solution, which you can identify manually.*

For example, let's say you have a problem statement: *find the total count of vowels from this book*. If you want to find the solution to this statement, what will you do?

The probable steps for the solution to this problem are as follows:

1. First, get the right book. I am assuming that you know the vowels (*a, e, i, o,* and *u*).

2. How many vowels did you find in a book?--0 (zero).

3. Open the current page (initially, our current page is 1) and start reading to find vowels.

4. If the letter matches *a, e, i, o,* or *u* (please note that the case doesn't matter, so the letters might as well be *A, E, I, O,* and *U*), then increase the vowel count by one.

5. Is the current page completed?

6. If the answer of step 5 is yes, then check if this is the last page of the book:

   - If yes, then we have the total vowel count in hand, which is nothing but *n*, where *n* is the total number of vowels found in the current chapter. Move to step 8 for the result.
   - If this is not the last chapter, move to the next chapter by adding 1 to the current chapter number. So, we should move to 1 + 1 = 2 (Chapter 2).

7. In the next chapter, repeat steps 4 to 6 and until you reach the last chapter of the book.

8. Finally, we have the total vowel count, that is, *n* (*n* is the total number of vowels found).

The preceding steps just described how we reached a perfect solution for our problem statement. These steps showed how we manually found the answer to our problem of counting all the vowels in the book's chapters.

In the programming world, such steps are collectively known as an *algorithm*.

An algorithm is nothing but a process to solve a problem by defining a set of rules.

When we write the preceding step(s)/algorithm in such a way that a machine/computer will be able to follow the instructions, it is called programming. These instructions should be written in a language understood by the machine/computer, and this is what is called a programming language.

In this book, we will use C# 7.0 as the programming language and .NET Core as the framework.

What is .NET?

While we are referring to .NET (pronounced as dot NET), it is .NET Full, as we have .NET Core in place and we are using .NET Core in our book examples with C# 7.0 as the language. Before moving ahead, you should know about .NET because there is a .NET Standard available with the .NET Core, that is API servers for both .NET Framework as well .NET Core. So, if you created a project using .NET Standard it is valid for both .NET Framework and .NET Core.

.NET is nothing but a combination of languages, runtime, and libraries, by using which we can develop managed software/applications. The software written in .NET is managed or is in a managed environment. To understand managed, we need to dig into how binary executables are available for operating systems. This comprises three broader steps:

1. Writing the code (source code).
2. Compiler compiles the source code.
3. The operating system executes the binary executable immediately:

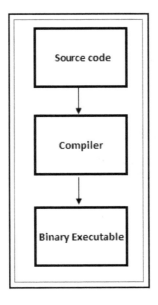

Broader steps – how binary executable is available?

The preceding process is a standard process depicting how compilers compile the source code and create executable binaries, but in the case of .NET, the compiler (C# compiler for our code) does not directly provide a binary executable; it provides an assembly and this assembly consists of metadata and intermediate language code, also known as **Microsoft Intermediate Language** (**MSIL**) or **Intermediate Language** (**IL**). This MSIL is a high-level language and this can't be understood directly by the machine, as MSIL is not machine-specific code or byte code. For proper execution, it should be interpreted. This interpretation from MSIL or IL to the machine language happens with the help of JIT. In other words, JIT compiles MSIL, IL into the machine language, also called native code. For more information, refer to `https://msdn.microsoft.com/en-us/library/ht8ecch6(v=vs.90).aspx`.

For 64-bit compilation, Microsoft has announced RyuJIT (`https://blogs.msdn.microsoft.com/dotnet/2014/02/27/ryujit-ctp2-getting-ready-for-prime-time/`). In the coming versions, 32-bit compilation will also be handled by RyuJIT (`https://github.com/dotnet/announcements/issues/10`). After this, we can now have a single code base for both CoreCLR.

 Intermediate language is a high-level component-based assembly language.

In our seven days of learning, we will not focus on the framework, but we will be more focused on the C# language with the use of .NET Core. In the coming sections, we will discuss important things of .NET Core in such a way that while we work with a C# program, we should understand how our program talks with the operating system.

What is .NET Core?

.NET Core is a new general-purpose development environment introduced by Microsoft to meet cross-platform requirements. .NET Core supports Windows, Linux, and OSX.

.NET Core is an open source software development framework released under MIT License and maintained by the Microsoft and .NET community on the GitHub (`https://github.com/dotnet/core`) repository.

.NET Core features

Here are some important features of .NET Core, that make .NET Core an important evolution step in software development:

- **Cross-platform**: Currently, .NET Core can be run on Windows, Linux, and macOS; in the future, there may be more. Refer to the roadmap (`https://github.com/dotnet/core/blob/master/roadmap.md`) for more info.
- **Having easy command-line tools**: You can use command-line tools for exercise with .NET Core. Refer to CLI tools for more at `https://docs.microsoft.com/en-us/dotnet/articles/core/tools/index`.
- **Having compatibility**: With the use of the .NET standard library, .NET Core is compatible with the .NET Frameworks, Xamarin and Mono.
- **Open source**: .NET Core platform is released under MIT License and is a .NET Foundation project (`https://dotnetfoundation.org/`).

What makes .NET Core?

.NET Core is a combination of **coreclr**, **corefx**, and **cli and roslyn**. These are the main components of .NET Core composition.

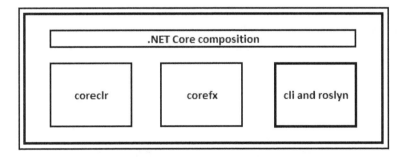

- **Coreclr**: It is a .NET runtime and provides assembly loading, garbage collector, and many more. You can check coreclr for more info at `https://github.com/dotnet/coreclr`.
- **Corefx**: It is a framework library; you can check corefx for more info at `https://github.com/dotnet/corefx`.
- **Cli**: It is nothing but a command-line interface tool and roslyn is the language compiler (the C# language in our case). Refer to cli (`https://github.com/dotnet/cli`) and Roslyn for more info at `https://github.com/dotnet/roslyn`.

What is .NET Standard?

The .NET Standard is a set of APIs that resolves the problems of code sharing while you're trying to write cross-platform applications. Currently, Microsoft is working on .NET Standard 2.0 to make it streamlined, and these standards will be implemented by all, that is, .NET Framework, .NET Core, and Xamarin. With the use of .NET Standard (that is a set of APIs), you are ensuring that your program and class library will be available for all targeted .NET Frameworks and .NET Core. In other words, .NET Standard will replace **Portable Class Libraries (PCL)**. For more information, refer to `https://blogs.msdn.microsoft.com/dotnet/2016/09/26/introducing-net-standard/`.

 The .NET Standard 2.0 repository is available at `https://github.com/dotnet/standard`.

Till now, you've got an idea of .NET Core and a few other things that help build cross-platform applications. In the coming sections, we will prepare the environment in order to start learning the C# language using Visual Studio 2017 (preferably the community edition).

Available IDEs and editors for C#

Integrated Development Environment (IDE) is nothing but software facilitating the development of applications. On the other hand, editors are basically meant to add/update predefined or new content. When we talk about the C# editor, we are referring to an editor that helps write C# programs. Some editors come with a lot of add-ons or plugins and can compile or run the programs.

We will use Visual Studio 2017 as our preferred C# IDE; however, there are a few more C# IDEs and editors you can go with:

1. **Visual Studio Code:** VS Code is an editor, and you can start by downloading it from `https://code.visualstudio.com/`. To start with VS Code, you need to install the C# extension from `https://marketplace.visualstudio.com/items?itemName=ms-vscode.csharp`.
2. **Cloud9:** It is a web browser-based IDE. You can start it for free by signing up at `https://c9.io/signup`.
3. **JetBrain Rider:** This is a cross-platform IDE by JetBrains. For more information, visit `https://www.jetbrains.com/rider/`.
4. **Zeus IDE:** This is an IDE designed for the Windows platform. You can start using Zeus from `https://www.zeusedit.com/index.html`.

5. **Text editor:** This is the way you can go without any installation; just use a text editor of your choice. I use Notepad++ (`https://notepad-plus-plus.org/download/v7.3.3.html`) and the **Command Line Interface** (**CLI**) to build code. Refer to `https://docs.microsoft.com/en-us/dotnet/articles/core/tools/` to know more about how to start with the CLI.

There may be more alternative IDEs and editors, but they are not as important to us.

Setting up the environment

In this section, we will see step by step how to initiate the installation of Visual Studio 2017 (preferably, the community edition) on Windows 10:

1. Go to `https://www.visualstudio.com/downloads/` (you can also get the benefits of Dev Essentials from `https://www.visualstudio.com/dev-essentials/`).

2. Download **Visual Studio Community** (`https://www.visualstudio.com/thank-you-downloading-visual-studio/?sku=Community&rel=15`):

3. Start the Visual Studio setup.

4. From **Workloads**, select the options you want to install. For our book, we need **.NET desktop development** and .NET Core:

5. Click on **Install** to start the installation:

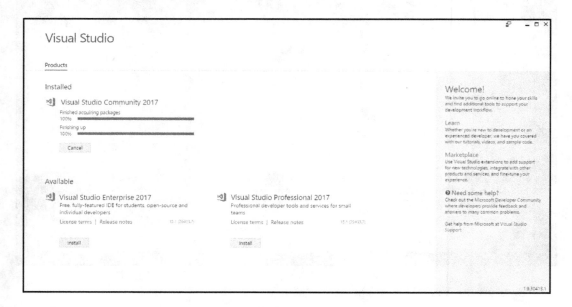

6. Click **Launch** once the installation is completed.
7. Sign up for Visual Studio using your Live ID.
8. Select **Visual C#** as your development setting.
9. You will see the start page as follows:

We are all set to start with our first step.

Hands - on exercises

Answer the following questions by covering the concepts of today's learning.

- What is programming? Write down an algorithm to find out vowel counts from all the pages of book, *Learn C# in 7-days*.
- What is .NET Core and .NET Standard?
- What makes a .NET Core an evolutional software ?

Revisiting Day 01

Today, we walked you through some important concepts of .NET Core and .NET Standard. You learned what programs and algorithms are in the programming world.

2
Day 02 - Getting Started with C#

Today, we are on day two of our seven-day learning series. Yesterday, we had gone through the basic understanding of .NET Core and its important aspects. Today, we will discuss the C# programming language. We will start with basics concepts by understanding a typical C# program, and then we will start looking at other stuff by covering reserved keywords, types, and operators; by the end of day, we will be able to write a complete C# program after covering the following topics:

- Introducing C#
- Understanding a typical C# program
- An overview of C# reserved keywords, types, and operators
- An overview of type conversion
- Understanding statements
- Arrays and string manipulations
- Structure versus class

Introduction to C#

In simple words, C# (pronounced *See-Sharp*) is a programming language that is developed by Microsoft. C# is approved by **International Standards Organization (ISO)** and **European Computer Manufacturers Association (ECMA)**.

This is the definition on the official website (`https://docs.microsoft.com/en-us/dotnet/csharp/tour-of-csharp/index`):

> *C# is a simple, modern, object-oriented, and type-safe programming language. C# has its roots in the C family of languages and will be immediately familiar to C, C++, Java, and JavaScript programmers.*

Language C# is designed to adhere to **Common Language Infrastructure** (**CLI**), which we discussed on day one.

C# is the most popular professional language because of the following reasons:

- It is an object-oriented language
- It is component-oriented
- It is a structured language
- The main part that makes it the most popular: this is a part of the .NET Framework
- It has a unified type system, which means all types of language C# inherits from a single type object (this is also known as the mother type)
- It was constructed with a robust durable application such as *Garbage collection* (discussed on day one)
- It has the ability to handle unknown issues within a program, which is known as exceptional handling (we will discuss exception handling on day four)
- Robust support of reflection, which enables dynamic programming (we will discuss reflection on day four)

History of the C# language

The C# language was developed by *Anders Hejlsberg* and his team. The language name is inspired by the musical notation *sharp* (#), which indicates that the written note should be made a semitone higher in pitch.

The first released version was C# 1.0, which was launched in January 2002, and the current version is C# 7.0.

The following table depicts all versions of the C# language.

Version of C#	Release year	Description
1.0	January 2002	With Visual Studio 2002 – .NET Framework 1.0
1.2	April 2003	With Visual Studio 2003 – .NET Framework 1.1
2.0	November 2005	With Visual Studio 2005 – .NET Framework 2.0
3.0	November 2007	Visual Studio 2008, Visual Studio 2010 – .NET Framework 3.0 and 3.5
4.0	April 2010	Visual Studio 2010 – .NET Framework 4
5.0	August 2012	Visual Studio 2012, 2013 – .NET Framework 4.5
6.0	July 2015	Visual Studio 2015 – .NET Framework 4.6
C# 7.0	March 2017	Visual Studio 2017 – .NET Framework 4.6.2
C# 7.1	August 2017	Visual Studio 2017 update3 – .NET Framework 4.7

In the upcoming section, we will discuss this language in detail, along with code examples. We will discuss C# language's keywords, types, operators, and so on.

Understanding a typical C# program

Before we start writing a program in C#, let's first go back to day one, where we discussed the various IDEs and editors that are helpful in writing programs/applications using the C# language. Revisit day one and understand various editors and IDEs and check why we should go with one of our choice. We will be using Visual Studio 2017 update 3 for all our examples in this book.

 To know the steps to install Visual Studio 2017, refer to `https://docs.` `microsoft.com/en-us/visualstudio/install/install-visual-studio.`

To get start with a simple C# program (we will create a console application), follow these steps:

1. Initiate your Visual Studio.
2. Go to **File** | **New** | **Project** (or *ctrl +Shift + N*).
3. Under **Visual C#** node, select **.NET Core** and then select **Console App**.
4. Name your program, say, Day02, and click on **OK** (see highlighted text in the following figure):

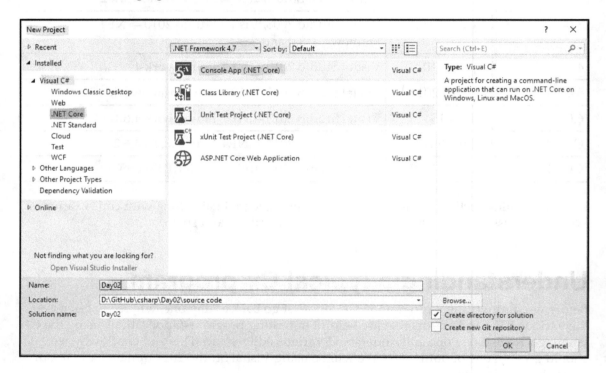

You will get the following code in class Program.cs – this is the default code provided by Visual Studio; you can amend it as per your need:

```
using System;

namespace Day02
{
class Program
    {
     static void Main(string[] args)
        {
```

```
        Console.WriteLine("Hello World!");
    }
}
}
```

By hitting the *F5* key on your keyboard, you will run the program in Debug mode.

 Typically, every program has two different configurations or modes, that is, Debug and Release. In Debug mode, all compiled files and symbols that are helpful to drill down any issue encountered during the execution of application will be loaded. On the other hand, Release is kind of a clean run, where only binaries without Debug symbols load and perform the action. For more information, refer to https://stackoverflow.com/questions/933739/what-is-the-difference-between-release-and-debug-modes-in-visual-studio.

You can see the following output when the program runs:

```
Hello World!
```

Before moving further, let's analyze the following figure of our console application on Visual Studio:

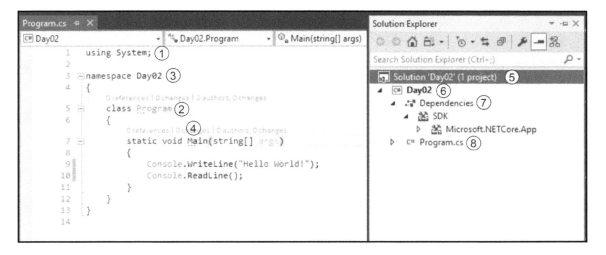

The preceding figure depicts a typical C# program; we are using Visual Studio, but the console program remains unchanged across different IDEs or editors. Let's discuss this in more detail.

1 (System)

This is a place where we defined what the namespaces going to be consumed in the program/application are. Generally, this is called using a statement, which includes the usage of external, internal, or any other namespaces.

System is a typical namespace that contains a lot of fundamental classes. For more information, refer to `https://docs.microsoft.com/en-us/dotnet/api/system?view=netcore-2.0`.

3 (Day02)

This is the namespace of our existing console application.

A namespace is a way to keep one set of names separate from another, which means you can create as many namespaces as you want and the classes under different namespaces will treat them as a separate, although they have the same name; that is, if you declare a `ClassExample` class in `namespace Day02`, it would be different from the `ClassExample` class declared in the `Day02New namespace` and will work without any conflicts.

This is a typical example that shows two classes of the same name with two different `namespaces`:

```
namespace Day02
{
public class ClassExample
    {
public void Display()
        {
Console.WriteLine("This is a class 'ClassExample' of namespace 'Day02'. ");
        }
    }
}

namespace Day02New
{

public class ClassExample
    {
public void Display()
        {
Console.WriteLine("This is a class 'ClassExample' of namespace 'Day02New'. ");
        }
```

```
    }
}
```

The preceding code would be called like this:

```
private static void SameClassDifferentNamespacesExample()
{
var class1 = new ClassExample();
var class2 = new Day02New.ClassExample();
    class1.Display();
    class2.Display();
}
```

This will return the following output:

```
Day02 - Leanr C# in 7-days
This is a class 'ClassExample' of namespace 'Day02'.
This is a class 'ClassExample' of namespace 'Day02New'.
```

2 (Program)

This is a class name defined in namespace - day two.

A class in C# is a blueprint of an object. Objects are dynamically created instances of a class. In our console program, we have a class program that contains a method named `Main`.

4 (Main)

This is an entry point for our program. At least one `Main` method is required for our C# program, and it should be static. We will discuss *static* in detail in the upcoming section, *Overview of C# reserved keywords*. `Main` is also a reserved keyword.

An entry is a way that lets CLR know the *what* and *where* of the functions located in the DLL. For instance, whenever we run our console application, it tells CLR that `Main` is the entry point and everything surrounds here. For more details, refer to `https://docs. microsoft.com/en-us/dotnet/framework/interop/specifying-an-entry-point` and `https://docs.microsoft.com/en-us/dotnet/framework/interop/specifying-an-entry-point`.

5 (Day02)

This is the name of the solution of our console application.

A solution can contain many libraries, applications, projects, and so on. For instance, our solution, **Day02**, would contain another project called Day03 or Day04. A Visual Studio solution filename for our console application is `Day02.sln`.

Refer to `https://stackoverflow.com/questions/30601187/what-is-a-solution-in-visual-studio` in order to understand the Visual Studio solution.

 To view the solution file, open the folder where `Day02.sln` solution file is located. You can directly open this file using any text editor/Notepad. I used Notepad++ (`https://notepad-plus-plus.org/`) to view the solution file.

The following screenshot depicts our solution file:

```
Microsoft Visual Studio Solution File, Format Version 12.00
# Visual Studio 15
VisualStudioVersion = 15.0.26730.3
MinimumVisualStudioVersion = 10.0.40219.1
Project("{FAE04EC0-301F-11D3-BF4B-00C04F79EFBC}") = "Day02", "Day02\Day02.csproj", "{9C67DB5B-DD9D-45AB-BF0B-99563676FEB2}"
EndProject
Global
	GlobalSection(SolutionConfigurationPlatforms) = preSolution
		Debug|Any CPU = Debug|Any CPU
		Release|Any CPU = Release|Any CPU
	EndGlobalSection
	GlobalSection(ProjectConfigurationPlatforms) = postSolution
		{9C67DB5B-DD9D-45AB-BF0B-99563676FEB2}.Debug|Any CPU.ActiveCfg = Debug|Any CPU
		{9C67DB5B-DD9D-45AB-BF0B-99563676FEB2}.Debug|Any CPU.Build.0 = Debug|Any CPU
		{9C67DB5B-DD9D-45AB-BF0B-99563676FEB2}.Release|Any CPU.ActiveCfg = Release|Any CPU
		{9C67DB5B-DD9D-45AB-BF0B-99563676FEB2}.Release|Any CPU.Build.0 = Release|Any CPU
	EndGlobalSection
	GlobalSection(SolutionProperties) = preSolution
		HideSolutionNode = FALSE
	EndGlobalSection
	GlobalSection(ExtensibilityGlobals) = postSolution
		SolutionGuid = {C9765BF5-31DE-44B8-893F-5E8DE50E7B19}
	EndGlobalSection
EndGlobal
```

6 (Day02)

This is a project of our console application.

A project is a bundle that contains everything required for your program. This is the definition of the project from the official website: https://docs.microsoft.com/en-us/visualstudio/ide/solutions-and-projects-in-visual-studio

> *A project is contained, in a logical sense and in the file system, within a solution, which may contain one or more projects, along with build information,Visual Studio window settings and any miscellaneous files that aren't associated with any project. In a literal sense, the solution is a text file with its own unique format; it is generally not intended to be edited by hand.*

Our project filename is Day02.csproj.

You are not required to have a project for your application. You can directly start working on your C# files.

The following screenshot depicts our project file:

```
<Project Sdk="Microsoft.NET.Sdk">

  <PropertyGroup>
    <OutputType>Exe</OutputType>
    <TargetFramework>netcoreapp2.0</TargetFramework>
  </PropertyGroup>

</Project>
```

7 (Dependencies)

This refers to all references and binaries required to run a specific application.

Dependency is an assembly or dll on which our application depends or where our application is consuming the function of referred assembly. For instance, our console application requires .NET Core 2.0 SDK, so it includes it as dependencies. Refer to the following screenshot:

8 (Program.cs)

This is physical class filename.

This is the name of a class file that is physically available on our disk drive. Class name and filename could be different, which means if my class name is `Program`, then my class filename could be `Program1.cs`. However, it is bad practice to call both class and filename with different names, but you can do that and the compiler won't throw any exception. For more information, refer to `https://stackoverflow.com/questions/2224653/c-sharp-cs-file-name-and-class-name-need-to-be-matched`.

Deep-dive into application using Visual Studio

In the previous section, you learned about various things that our console application can contain. In this section, lets deep-dive to get more insight on this using Visual Studio.

To get started, go to the project properties. Do this from the solution explorer (right-click on project and click on **Properties**) or from menus (**Project | Day02** properties); you will get the project properties window, as shown in the following screenshot:

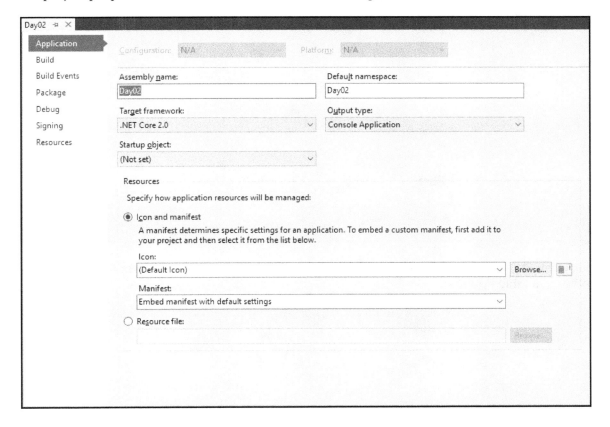

On the **Application** tab, we can set the **Assembly name**, the **Default namespace**, the **Target framework**, and the **Output type** (the output types are `Console Application`, `Windows Application`, `Class Library`).

The following screenshot is that of the **Build** tab:

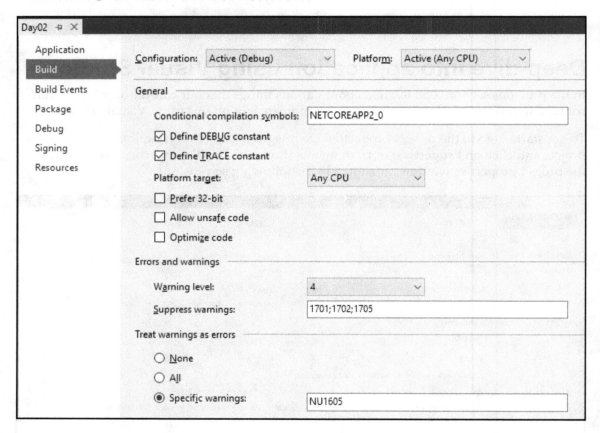

From the **Build** tab, we can set **Conditional compilation symbols**, **Platform target**, and other available options.

Conditional compilations are nothing but pre-processors, which we will discuss on day six.

The following screenshot depicts the **Package** tab:

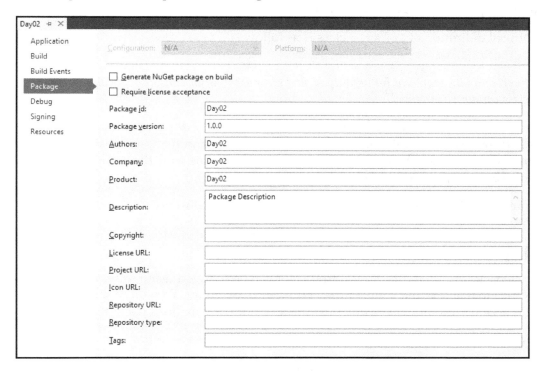

The **Package** tab helps us directly create NuGet packages. In the earlier version, we needed a lot of configuration settings to build a NuGet package. In the current version, we just need to provide the information on the **Package** tab, and Visual Studio will generate the NuGet package according to our options. The **Debug** tab, **Signing,** and **Resources** tabs are self-explanatory and provide us with a way to sign assemblies and support to embed resources in our program.

Discussing code

We have gone through the console application and discussed what a typical console application contains and how we can set various things using Visual Studio. Now let's discuss our code, which was written in the previous section, *Understanding a typical C# program*.

`Console` is a static class of a `System` namespace and it can't be inherited.

In the said code, we instructed the program to write something to the console as an output with the help of the `WriteLine()` method.

The official definition of `Console` class is as follows (https://docs.microsoft.com/en-us/dotnet/api/system.console?view=netcore-2.0):

> *Represents the standard input, output, and error streams for console applications. This class cannot be inherited.*

`Console` is nothing but an operating system's terminal-windows (also known as **Console User Interface** (**CUI**))to interact with users. Windows operating system has console, that is, Command Prompt that accepts MS-DOS commands. In this way, the `Console` class provides basic support to achieve this.

Here are a few important operations we can do with the console.

Color

Console background and/or foreground color can be changed using setter and getter properties that accept the value of the `ConsoleColor` enum. To set it to the default color, there is a `Reset` method. Let's demonstrate all color combinations using the following code:

```
private static (int, int) DisplayColorMenu(ConsoleColor[] colors)
{
var count = 0;

foreach (var color in colors)
    {
        WriteLine($"{count}{color}");
        count += 1;
    }
WriteLine($"{count + 1} Reset");
WriteLine($"{count + 2} Exit");

Write("Choose Foreground color:");
var foreground = Convert.ToInt32(ReadLine());
Write("Choose Background color:");
var background = Convert.ToInt32(ReadLine());

return new ValueTuple<int, int>(background, foreground);
}
```

The preceding code is one snippet from the complete source code that is available on the GitHub repository. The complete code will provide the following output:

```
Day02 - Leanr C# in 7-days
Console Color example

All available colors
0 Black
1 DarkBlue
2 DarkGreen
3 DarkCyan
4 DarkRed
5 DarkMagenta
6 DarkYellow
7 Gray
8 DarkGray
9 Blue
10 Green
11 Cyan
12 Red
13 Magenta
14 Yellow
15 White
17 Reset
18 Exit
Choose Foreground color:0
Choose Background color:9
Foreground color is Black
Background color is Blue

Type anything to see the change:This is a BLUE color
```

Beep

`Beep` is the method that generates system sound through the console speaker. The following is the simplest example:

```
private static void ConsoleBeepExample()
{
for (int i = 0; i < 9; i++)
Beep();
}
```

There are a few more methods that are helpful while working with the console application. For more detail on these methods, refer to `https://docs.microsoft.com/en-us/dotnet/api/system.console?view=netcore-2.0`.

Until now, we have discussed a typical C# program with the help of a code example using Visual Studio 2017; we went through various sections of the console program and discussed them. You can revisit this section once again or proceed with further reading.

An overview of C# reserved keywords, types, and operators

Reserved keywords are nothing but predefined words that have special meaning for the compilers. You cannot use these reserved keywords as normal text or identifiers unless you explicitly tell the compiler that this word is not meant to reserve for the compiler.

 In C#, you can use the reserved keyword as a normal word by prefixing the @ symbol.

C# keywords are divided into the following categories:

- **Types**: In C#, the typing system is divided into value type, reference type, and pointer type.
- **Modifiers**: As is self-explanatory from its name, modifiers are used to modify the declaration of types and members of a specific type.
- **Statement keywords**: These are programming instructions that execute in a sequence.
- **Method parameters**: These can be declared as a value type or a ref type and values can be passed using **out** or **ref** keywords.
- **Namespace keywords**: These are the keywords that belong to namespaces only.
- **Operator keywords**: These operators are generally used to perform miscellaneous operations, such as type checking, getting the size of the object, and so on.
- **Conversion keywords**: These are `explicit`, `implicit`, and `operator` keywords, which will be discussed in the upcoming sections.
- **Access keywords**: These are common keywords that help access things from a class that belongs to its parent class or belongs to its own. These keywords are `this` and `base`.
- **Literal keywords**: Keywords have some values for assignment, which are `null`, `true`, `false`, and `default`.
- **Contextual keywords**: These are used as a specific meaning in the code. These are special keywords that are not reserved keywords in C#.
- **Query keywords**: These are contextual keywords that can be used in a query expression, for instance, the `from` keyword can be used for LINQ.

In the upcoming sections, we will discuss C# keywords in more detail using code examples.

Identifiers

These keywords are used in any part of the C# program and are reserved. Identifiers are special keywords and are treated differently by the compiler.

These are the identifiers that are reserved by C#:

- **abstract**: This informs you that things that come with the abstract modifier are yet to complete or have a missing definition. We will discuss this in detail on day four.
- **as**: This can be used in a cast operation. In other words, we can say that this checks the compatibility between two types.

 The as keyword falls in the operator category of keywords; refer to https://docs.microsoft.com/en-us/dotnet/csharp/language-reference/keywords/operator-keywords.

The following is the small code snippet that demonstrates the as identifier:

```
public class Stackholder
{
public void GetAuthorName(Person person)
    {
var authorName = person as Author;
Console.WriteLine(authorName != null ? $"Author is {authorName.Name}" :"No
author.");
    }

}

//Rest code is omitted
```

The preceding code snippet has a method that writes the name of an author to the console window. With the help of the as operator, it is called by the following code:

```
private static void ExampleIsAsOperator()
{
WriteLine("isas Operator");
var author = new Author{Name = "Gaurav Aroraa"};

WriteLine("Author name using as:\n");
stackholder.GetAuthorName(author);

}
```

This will produce the following result:

```
Day02 - Leanr C# in 7-days
Is As Operator
Author name using as:

Author is Gaurav Aroraa
```

- **base**: This is the access keyword and is used to access members of the parent class from within derived classes. The following is the code snippet that shows the usage of the base keyword. For more information, refer to https://docs. microsoft.com/en-us/dotnet/csharp/language-reference/keywords/base

```csharp
public class TeamMember :Person
{
public override string Name { get; set; }
public void GetMemberName()
    {
    Console.WriteLine($"Member name:{Name}");
    }
}

public class ContentMember :TeamMember
{
public ContentMember(string name)
    {
    base.Name = name;
    }
public void GetContentMemberName()
    {
    base.GetMemberName();
    }
}
```

This is a very simple example used to showcase the power of base. Here, we are just using base class members and methods to get the expected output:

- **bool**: This is an alias of structureSystem.Boolean that helps declare variables. This has two values: true or false. We will discuss this in detail in the upcoming section, *Data types*.
- **break**: The keyword is self-explanatory; it breaks something within a particular code execution, which could be a flow statement (for loop) or the termination of a code block (switch). We will discuss this in detail in the upcoming section on loop and statements.

- **byte**: This helps declare variables of an unsigned integer. This is an alias of `System.Byte`. We will discuss this in detail in the upcoming section.
- **case**: This is used with the `Switch` statement, which then tends to a code block of execution based on some condition. We will discuss `switch` case on day three.
- **catch**: This keyword is a catch block of exception handling blocks, that is, `try..catch..finally`. We will discuss exception handling in detail on day six.
- **char**: This keyword is useful when we declare a variable to store characters that belong to structure `System.Char`. We will discuss this in detail in the data type section.
- **checked**: Sometimes, you might face overflow values in your program. Overflow exception means that you assigned a larger value than the max value of the assignee data type. The compiler raises the overflow exception and the program terminates. The keyword checks force the compiler to make sure that overflow will not happen to the scenario when the compiler misses it. To understand this better, look at the following code snippet:

```
int sumWillthrowError = 2147483647 + 19; //compile time error
```

This will generate a compile-time error. As soon as you write the preceding statement, you get the following error:

```
int sumWillthrowError = 2147483647 + 19; //compile time error

        The operation overflows at compile time in checked mode

        Overflow in constant value computation
```

The following code snippet is a modified code, as shown in the preceding figure. With this modification, the new code will not generate a compile-time error:

```
Private static void CheckOverFlowExample()
{
var maxValue = int.MaxValue;
var addSugar = 19;
var sumWillNotThrowError = maxValue + addSugar;
WriteLine($"sum value:{sumWillNotThrowError} is not the correct value
because it is larger than {maxValue}.");
}
```

The preceding code will never throw an overflow exception, but it would not give the correct sum; it gives **-2147483647** as a result of 2147483647 + 19 because the actual sum will exceed the maximum positive value of an integer, that is, 2147483647. It will produce the following output:

```
Day02 - Learn C# in 7-days
sum value:-2147483630 is not the correct value because it is larger than 2147483647.
```

In real-world programs, we can't take a risk with wrong calculations. We should use the checked keyword to overcome such situations. Let's rewrite the preceding code using checked keywords:

```
private static void CheckOverFlowExample()
{
const int maxValue = int.MaxValue;
const int addSugar = 19;
var sumWillNotThrowError = checked(maxValue+addSugar); //compile time error
WriteLine(
$"sum value:{sumWillNotThrowError} is not the correct value because it is
larger than {maxValue}.");
}
```

As soon as you write the code using the **checked** keyword, you will see the following compile-time error:

```
var sumWillNotThrowError = checked(maxValue + addSugar); //compile time error
                                   The operation overflows at compile time in checked mode

                                   Overflow in constant value computation
```

Now let's discuss more keywords of C#:

- **class**: This keyword helps us declare classes. A C# class would contain members, methods, variables, fields, and so on (we will discuss these in detail on day four). Classes are different from structures; we will discuss this in detail in the *Classes versus structures* section.
- **const**: This keyword helps us declare constant fields or constant locals. We will discuss this in detail on day three.

- **continue**: This keyword is the opponent of `break`. It passes control to the next iteration in the flow statements, that is, `while`, `do`, `for`, and `foreach`. We will discuss this in detail in the upcoming sections.
- **decimal**: This helps us declare a data type of 128-bit. We will discuss this in detail in the *Data types* section.
- **default**: This is the keyword that tells us the default condition in a `switch` statement. We can also use the default as a literal to get the default values; we will discuss this on day three.
- **delegate**: This helps declare a delegate type that is similar to method signature. We will discuss this in detail on day six.
- **do**: This executes a statement repeatedly until it meets the expression condition of false. We will discuss this in the upcoming section.
- **double**: This helps declare simple 64-bit floating point values. We will discuss this in detail in the upcoming section.
- **else**: This comes with the `if` statement and executes the `code` statement that does not fall within the `if` condition. We will discuss this in detail in the coming section.
- **enum**: This helps create enumerations. We will discuss this on day four.
- **event**: This helps declare an event in a publisher class. We will discuss this in detail on day six.
- **explicit**: This is one of the conversion keywords. This keyword declares a user-defined type conversion operator. We will discuss this in detail in the upcoming section.
- **false**: A bool value indicates the `false` condition, `result`, or `Operator`. We will discuss this in detail in the upcoming sections.
- **finally**: This is a part of exception handling blocks. Finally, a block is always executed. We will discuss this in detail on day four.
- **fixed**: This is used in unsafe code and is helpful in preventing GC allocation or relocation. We will discuss this in detail on day six.
- **float**: This is a simple data type that stores a 32-bit floating point value. We will discuss this in detail in the upcoming section.
- **for**: The `for` keyword is a part of flow statements. With the use of the `for` loop, you can run a statement repeatedly until a specific expression is reached. We will discuss this in detail in the upcoming section.
- **foreach**: This is also a flow statement, but it works only on elements for collections or arrays. This can be exited using the `goto`, `return`, `break`, and `throw` keywords. We will discuss this in detail in the upcoming section.

- **goto**: This redirects the control to another part with the help of a label. In C#, goto is typically used with the `switch..case` statement. We will discuss this in detail in the upcoming sections.

- **if**: This is a conditional statement keyword. It typically comes with the `if...else` statement. We will discuss this in detail in the upcoming sections.

- **implicit**: Similar to the explicit keyword, this helps declare an implicit user-defined conversion. We will discuss this in detail in the upcoming sections.

- **in**: A keyword helps detect the collection from where we need to iterate through members in the `foreach` loop. We will discuss this in detail in the upcoming sections.

- **int**: This is an alias of structure `System.Int32` and a data type that stores signed 32-bit integer values. We will discuss this in detail in the upcoming sections.

- **interface**: This keyword helps declare an interface that can only contain methods, properties, events, and indexers (we will discuss this on day four).

- **internal**: This is an access modifier. We will discuss this in detail on day four.

- **is**: Similar to the `as` operator, `is` is also a keyword operator.

- This is a code example showing the `is` operator:

```csharp
public void GetStackholdersname(Person person)
{
if (person is Author)
    {
    Console.WriteLine($"Author name:{((Author)person).Name}");
    }
elseif (person is Reviewer)
    {
    Console.WriteLine($"Reviewer name:{((Reviewer)person).Name}");
    }
elseif(person is TeamMember)
    {
    Console.WriteLine($"Member name:{((TeamMember)person).Name}");
    }
else
    {
    Console.Write("Not a valid name.");
    }

}
```

For complete explanation of `is` and `as` operators, refer to `https://goo.gl/4n73JC`.

- **lock**: This represents a critical section of the code block. With the use of the `lock` keyword, we will get a mutual exclusion lock of an object, and it will get released after execution of the statement. This generally comes with the use of threading. Threading is beyond the scope of this book. For more details, refer to `https://docs.microsoft.com/en-us/dotnet/csharp/language-reference/keywords/lock-statement` and `https://docs.microsoft.com/en-us/dotnet/csharp/programming-guide/concepts/threading/index`.
- **long**: This helps declare variables to store signed 64-bit integers values, and it refers to structure `System.Int64`. We will discuss this in detail in the upcoming sections.
- **namespace**: This helps define namespaces that declare a set of related objects. We will discuss this in details on day four.
- **new**: The `new` keyword can be an operator, a modifier, or a constraint. We will discuss this in detail on day four.
- **null**: This represents a null reference. It does not refer to any object. The default value of reference type is null. This is helpful while working with nullable types.
- **object**: This is an alias of `System.Object`, the universal type in .NET world. It accepts any data type instead of null.
- **operator**: This helps overload the built-in operator. We will discuss this in detail in the upcoming sections..
- **out**: This is a contextual keyword and will be discussed in detail on day four.
- **override**: This keyword helps override or extend the implementation of abstract or virtual members, methods, properties , indexer, or event. We will discuss this in detail on day four.
- **params**: This helps define method parameters with a variable number of arguments. We will discuss this in detail on day four.
- **private**: This is an access modifier and will be discussed on day four.
- **protected**: This is an access modifier and will be discussed on day four.
- **public**: This is an access modifier that sets the availability through the application and will be discussed on day four.
- **readonly**: This helps us declare field declaration as read-only. We will discuss this in detail on day four.
- **ref**: This helps pass values by reference. We will discuss this in detail on day four.
- **return**: This helps terminate the execution of a method and returns the result for the calling method. We will discuss this in detail on day four.

- **sbyte**: This denotes `System.SByte` and stores signed 8-bit integer values. We will discuss this in detail in the upcoming sections.
- **sealed**: This is a modifier that prevents further usage/extension. We will discuss this in detail on day four.
- **short**: This denotes `System.Int16` and stores signed 16-bit integer values. We will discuss this in detail in the upcoming sections.
- **sizeof**: This helps get the size in bytes of the inbuilt type and/or unmanaged type. For unmanaged and all other types apart from inbuilt data types, the unsafe keyword is required.
- The following code is explained `sizeof` using built-in types:

```
private static void SizeofExample()
{
WriteLine("Various inbuilt types have size as mentioned below:\n");
WriteLine($"The size of data type int is: {sizeof(int)}");
WriteLine($"The size of data type long is: {sizeof(long)}");
WriteLine($"The size of data type double is: {sizeof(double)}");
WriteLine($"The size of data type bool is: {sizeof(bool)}");
WriteLine($"The size of data type short is: {sizeof(short)}");
WriteLine($"The size of data type byte is: {sizeof(byte)}");
}
```

The preceding code produces the following output:

```
Day02 - Learn C# in 7-days
Various inbuilt types have size as mentioned below:

The size of data type int is: 4
The size of data type long is: 8
The size of data type double is: 8
The size of data type bool is: 1
The size of data type short is: 2
The size of data type byte is: 1
```

Let's discuss more C# keywords; these keywords are very important and play a vital role while writing real-world programs:

- **static**: This helps us declare static members and will be discussed in detail on day four.
- **string**: This helps store unicode characters. It is a reference type. We will be discussing this in more detail in the upcoming section, *String*.

- **struct**: This helps us declare a `struct` type. Struct type is a value type. We will be discussing this in more detail in the upcoming section, *Classes versus. structs*.

- **switch**: This helps declare a `switch` statement. Switch is a selection statement, and we will be discussing it on day three.

- **this**: This `this` keyword helps us access the members of the current instance of a class. It is also a modifier and we will be discussing on day four. Note that the `this` keyword has a special meaning for the `extension` method. Extension methods are beyond the scope of this book; refer to `https://docs.microsoft.com/en-us/dotnet/csharp/programming-guide/classes-and-structs/extension-methods` for more detail.

- **throw**: This helps throw a system or custom exceptions. We will be discussing this in detail on day six.

- **true**: Similar to false, we discussed this earlier. It represents a Boolean value and can be a literal or operator. We will discuss this in more detail in the upcoming section.

- **try**: This represents a `try` block of exception handling. Try block is one of the other three blocks that helps handle any unavoidable errors or instances of programs. All three blocks are jointly called exceptional handling blocks. The try block always comes first. This block contains the code that could throw an exception. We will discuss this in more detail on day six.

- **typeof**: This helps get the type object for a desired type. Also, at runtime, you can get the type of object with the help of the `GetType()` method.

The following code snippet shows the `typeof()` method in action:

```
private static void TypeofExample()
{
var thisIsADouble = 30.3D;
WriteLine("using typeof()");
WriteLine($"System.Type Object of {nameof(Program)} is
{typeof(Program)}\n");
var objProgram = newProgram();
WriteLine("using GetType()");
WriteLine($"Sytem.Type Object of {nameof(objProgram)} is
{objProgram.GetType()}");
WriteLine($"Sytem.Type Object of {nameof(thisIsADouble)} is
{thisIsADouble.GetType()}");
}
```

The preceding code will generate the following result:

```
Day02 - Learn C# in 7-days
using typeof()
System.Type Object of Program is Day02.Program

using GetType()
Sytem.Type Object of objProgram is Day02.Program
Sytem.Type Object of thisIsADouble is System.Double
```

These are the unsigned data types, and these data types store values without sign (+/-):

- **uint**: This helps declare a variable of an unsigned 32-bit integer. We will be discussing this in detail in the upcoming section.
- **ulong**: This helps declare a variable of an unsigned 65-bit integer. We will be discussing this in detail in the upcoming section.
- **unchecked**: This keyword works exactly opposite to checked. The code block that threw a compile-time error with the use of the checked keyword will not generate any compile-time exception with the use of the unchecked keyword.
  Let's rewrite the code that we wrote using the checked keyword and see how the unchecked keyword works exactly opposite to checked:

```
private static void CheckOverFlowExample()
{
const int maxValue = int.MaxValue;
const int addSugar = 19;
//int sumWillthrowError = 2147483647 + 19; //compile time error
var sumWillNotThrowError = unchecked(maxValue+addSugar);
//var sumWillNotThrowError = checked(maxValue + addSugar);
//compile time error
WriteLine(
$"sum value:{sumWillNotThrowError} is not the correct value
because it is larger than {maxValue}.");
}
```

The preceding code will run smoothly but will give the wrong result, that is, **-2147483647**.

You can find more detail on the checked and unchecked keywords by referring to `https://docs.microsoft.com/en-us/dotnet/csharp/language-reference/keywords/checked`.

- **unsafe**: This helps execute an unsafe code block that generally uses pointers. We will be discussing this in detail on day six.
- **ushort**: This helps declare a variable of an unsigned 16-bit integer. We will be discussing this in more detail in the upcoming section, *Data types*.

- **using**: The using keyword works like a directive or statement. Let's consider the following code example:

```
using System;
```

The preceding directive provides everything that belongs to the System namespace:

```
using static System.Console;
```

The preceding directive helps us call static members. After inclusion of the preceding directive in the program, we can directly call static members, methods, and so on, as shown in the following code:

```
Console.WriteLine("This WriteLien is without using static directive");
WriteLine("This WriteLien is called after using static directive");
```

In the preceding code snippet, in first statement, we called Console.WriteLine, but in the second statement, there is no need to write the class name, so we can directly call the WriteLine method.

On the other hand, the using statement helps us perfectly use the IDisposable classes. The following code snippet tells us how a using statement is helpful while we are working with disposable classes (these classes use the IDisposable interface):

```
public class DisposableClass : IDisposable
{
public string GetMessage()
    {
     return"This is from a Disposable class.";
    }
protected virtual void Dispose(bool disposing)
    {
     if (disposing)
        {
         //disposing code here
        }
    }

public void Dispose()
    {
        Dispose(true);
        GC.SuppressFinalize(this);
    }
}
private static void UsingExample()
{
using (var disposableClass = new DisposableClass())
```

```
    {
     WriteLine($"{disposableClass.GetMessage()}");
    }
}
```

The preceding code produces the following output:

```
Day02 - Learn C# in 7-days
This is from a Disposable class.
```

C# keywords virtual and void have a special meaning: one allows the other to override it, while the other is a used as a return type when the method returns nothing. Let's discuss both in detail:

- **virtual**: If the virtual keyword is used, it means that it allows methods, properties, indexers, or events to override in a derived class. We will be discussing this in more detail on day four.
- **void**: This is an alias of the `System.Void` type. When void uses the method, it means the method does not have any return type. For instance, take a look at the following code snippet:

```
public void GetAuthorName(Person person)
{
var authorName = person as Author;
Console.WriteLine(authorName != null ? $"Author is {authorName.Name}" :"No
author.");
}
```

In the preceding code snippet, the `getAuthorName()` method is of void type; hence, it does not return anything.

- **while**: While is a flow statement that executes the specific code block until a specified expression evaluates false. We will be discussing this in more detail in the upcoming section, *Flow statements*.

Contextual

These are not reserved keywords, but they have a special meaning for a limited context of a program and can also be used as an identifier outside that context.

These are the contextual keywords of C#:

- **add**: This is used to define a custom accessor and it invokes when someone subscribes to an event. The `add` accessors are always followed by the `remove` accessors, which means when we provide the add accessor, the remove accessor should be applied thereon. For more information, refer to `https://docs.microsoft.com/en-us/dotnet/csharp/programming-guide/events/how-to-implement-interface-events`.
- **ascending/descending**: This contextual keyword is used with an `orderby` clause in a `LINQ` statement. We will discuss this in more detail on day six.
- **async**: This is used for an asynchronous method, lambda expression, or anonymous method. To get the result from asynchronous methods, the `await` keyword is used. We will be discussing this in more detail on day six.
- **dynamic**: This helps us bypass the compile-time type checking. This resolves types at runtime.

 Compile time type is what you used to define a variable. Runtime type refers to the actual type to which a variable belongs.

Let's look at the following code in order to understand these terms better:

```
internal class Parent
{
//stuff goes here
}
internal class Child : Parent
{
//stuff goes here
}
```

We can create an object of our child class like this:

```
Parent myObject = new Child();
```

Here, compile-time type for `myObject` is `Parent` as the compiler knows the variable is a type of `Parent` without caring or knowing about the fact that we are instantiate this object with type `Child`. Hence this is a compile-time type. Runtime type is the actual type that is `Child` in our example. Hence, runtime type of our variable `myObject` is `Child`.

Take a look at the following code snippet:

```
private static void DynamicTypeExample()
{
```

```
dynamic dynamicInt = 10;
dynamic dynamicString = "This is a string";
object obj = 10;
WriteLine($"Run-time type of {nameof(dynamicInt)} is
{dynamicInt.GetType()}");
WriteLine($"Run-time type of {nameof(dynamicString)} is
{dynamicString.GetType()}");
WriteLine($"Run-time type of {nameof(obj)} is {obj.GetType()}");

}
```

The above code produces following output:

```
Day02 - Learn C# in 7-days
Run-time type of dynamicInt is System.Int32
Run-time type of dynamicString is System.String
Run-time type of obj is System.Int32
```

For more information, refer: `https://docs.microsoft.com/en-us/dotnet/csharp/language-reference/keywords/dynamic`.

These are the contextual keywords that are used in query expressions; let's discuss these keywords in detail:

- **from**: This uses the in query expression and will be discussed on day six.
- **get**: This defines the accessor and is used along with properties for the retrieval of values. We will be discussing this in more detail on day six.
- **group**: This is used with a query expression and returns a sequence of `IGroupong<Tkey, TElement>` objects. We will discuss this in more detail on day six.
- **into**: This identifier helps store temporary data while working with query expressions. We will discuss this in more detail on day six.

For more information on contextual keywords, refer to `https://docs.microsoft.com/en-us/dotnet/csharp/language-reference/keywords`.

Types

In C#, 7.0 types are also known as data types and variables. These are categorized into the following broader categories.

Value type

These are derived from the `System.ValueType` class. Variables of the value type directly contains their data or, in simple words, the value type variable can be assigned directly. Value types can be divided into more sub categories: data types, custom types (`Enum` types and `Struct` types). In this section, we will discuss the data types in detail. `Enum` will be discussed on day four and struct will be discussed in the upcoming sections.

Data types

These are also famous as compliant value types, simple value types, and basic value types. I call these data types because of their power to define the nature of values. The following table contains all value types:

Nature	Type	CLR Type	Range	Default Value	Size
Signed Integer	sbyte	System.SByte	-128 to 127	0	8 bit
	short	System.Short	-32,768 to 32,767	0	16 bit
	int	System.Int32	-2,147,483,648 to 2,147,483,647	0	32 bit
	long	System.Int64	-9,223,372,036,854,775,808 to 9,223,372,036,854,775,807	0L	64 bit
Unsigned Integer	byte	System.Byte	0 to 255	0	8 bit
	ushort	System.UInt16	0 to 65,535	0	16 bit
	uint	System.UInt32	0 to 4,294,967,295	0	32 bit
	ulong	System.UInt64	0 to 18,446,744,073,709,551,615	0	64 bit
Unicode Character	char	System.Char	U +0000 to U +ffff	'\0'	16 bit
Floating point	float	System.Float	-3.4×10^{38} to $+ 3.4 \times 10^{38}$	0.0F	32 bit
	double	System.Double	$(+/-)5.0 \times 10^{-324}$ to $(+/-)1.7 \times 10^{308}$	0.0D	64 bit

| Higher-precision decimal | decimal | System.Decimal | (-7.9 x 1028 to 7.9 x 1028) / 100 to 28 | 0.0M | 128 bit |
| Boolean | bool | System.Boolean | True or False | False | Boolean value |

We can prove the values mentioned in the preceding table with the help of the following code snippet:

```
//Code is omitted
public static void Display()
{
WriteLine("Table :: Data Types");
var dataTypes = DataTypes();
WriteLine(RepeatIt('\u2500', 100));
WriteLine("{0,-10} {1,-20} {2,-50} {3,-5}", "Type", "CLR Type", "Range",
"Default Value");
WriteLine(RepeatIt('\u2500', 100));
foreach (var dataType in dataTypes)
WriteLine("{0,-10} {1,-20} {2,-50} {3,-5}", dataType.Type,
dataType.CLRType, dataType.Range,
dataType.DefaultValue);
WriteLine(RepeatIt('\u2500', 100));
}
//Code is omitted
```

In the preceding code, we are displaying maximum and minimum values of data types, which produces the following output:

```
Day02 - Learn C# in 7-days
Table :: Data Types

Type       CLR Type           Range                                              Default Value

sbyte      System.SByte       -128 to 127                                        0
short      System.Int16       -32768 to 32767                                    0
int        System.Int32       -2147483648 to 2147483647                          0
long       System.Int64       -9.223372E+018 to 9.223372E+018                    0L
byte       System.Byte        0 to 255                                           0
ushort     System.UInt16      0 to 65535                                         0
uint       System.UInt32      0 to 4294967295                                    0
ulong      System.UInt64      0 to 18446744073709551615                          0
char       System.Char        U +0000 to  U +ffff                                \0
float      System.Single      -3.402823E+038 to 3.402823E+038                    0.0F
double     System.Double      -1.797693E+308 to 1.797693E+308                    0.0D
decimal    System.Decimal     -7.92E+028 to 7.92E+028                            0.0M
bool       System.Boolean     True to False                                      False
```

Reference type

The actual data is not stored in the variable but it contains reference to variables. In simple words, we can say that the reference type refers to a memory location. Also, multiple variables can refer to one memory location, and if any of these variables change the data to that location, all the variables would get the new values. Here are the built-in reference types:

- **class type**: A data structure that contains members, methods, properties, and so on. This is also called the object type as this inherits the universal classSystem.Object. In C# 7.0, class type supports single inheritance; we will discuss this in more detail on day seven.

 The object type can be assigned a value of any other type; an object is nothing but an alias of System.Object. In this context, any other type is meant to be a value type, reference type, predefined type, and user-defined type.

There is a concept called boxing and unboxing that happens once we deal with an object type. In general, whenever value type is converted into the object type, it is called boxing, and when object type is converted into a value type, it is called unboxing.

Take a look at the following code snippet:

```
private static void BoxingUnboxingExample()
{
int thisIsvalueTypeVariable = 786;
object thisIsObjectTypeVariable = thisIsvalueTypeVariable; //Boxing
thisIsvalueTypeVariable += 1;
    WriteLine("Boxing");
WriteLine($"Before boxing: Value of {nameof(thisIsvalueTypeVariable)}:
{thisIsvalueTypeVariable}");
WriteLine($"After boxing: Value of {nameof(thisIsObjectTypeVariable)}:
{thisIsObjectTypeVariable}");

thisIsObjectTypeVariable = 1900;
thisIsvalueTypeVariable = (int) thisIsObjectTypeVariable; //Unboxing
    WriteLine("Unboxing");
WriteLine($"Before Unboxing: Value of {nameof(thisIsObjectTypeVariable)}:
{thisIsObjectTypeVariable}");
WriteLine($"After Unboxing: Value of {nameof(thisIsvalueTypeVariable)}:
{thisIsvalueTypeVariable}");
 }
```

In the preceding code snippet, we defined boxing and unboxing, where boxing happened when a value type `thisIsvalueTypeVariable` variable is assigned to an object `thisIsObjectTypeVariable`. On the other hand, unboxing happened when we cast object variable `thisIsObjectTypeVariable` to our value type `thisIsvalueTypeVariable` variable with int. This is the output of the code:

```
Day02 - Learn C# in 7-days
Boxing
Before boxing: Value of thisIsvalueTypeVariable: 787
After boxing: Value of thisIsObjectTypeVariable: 786
Unboxing
Before Unboxing: Value of thisIsObjectTypeVariable: 1900
After Unboxing: Value of thisIsvalueTypeVariable: 1900
```

Here, we are going to discuss three important types, which are interface, string, and delegate type:

- **interface type**: This type is basically a contract that is meant to be implemented by whoever is going to use it. A class or struct may use one or more interface types. One interface type may be inherited from multiple other interface types. We will discuss this in more details on day seven.
- **delegate type**: This is a type that represents a reference to a method of a parameter list. Famously, delegates are known as function pointers (as defined in C++). Delegates are type- safe. We will discuss this in detail on day four.
- **string type**: This is an alias of `System.String`. This type allows you to assign any string value to variables. We will discuss this in detail in the upcoming sections.

Pointer type

This type belongs to unsafe code. The variable defined as a pointer type stores the memory address of another variable. We will discuss this in details on day six.

Null type

Nullable types are nothing but an instance of the `System.Nullable<T>` struct. The nullable type contains the same data range as that of its `ValueType` but with addition to a null value. Refer to the data type table where int has a range of **2147483648** to **2147483647** but `System.Nullable<int>` or `int?` has the same range in addition to null. This means you can do this: `int? nullableNum = null;`.

For more detail on nullable types, refer to `https://docs.microsoft.com/en-us/dotnet/csharp/programming-guide/nullable-types/`.

Operators

In C#, operators are nothing but mathematical or logical operators that tell the compiler to perform a specific operation. For instance, a multiplication (*) operator tells the compiler to multiply; on the other hand, the logical and (&&) operator checks both the operands. We can divide C# operators into broader types, as shown in the following table:

Type	Operator	Description
Arithmetic operators	+	Adds two operands, for example, `var result = num1 +num2;`
	-	Subtracts second operand from first operand, for example, `var result = num1 - num2;`
	*	Multiplies both operands, for example, `var result = num1 * num2;`
	/	Divides the numerator by the denominator, for example, `var result = num1 / num2;`
	%	Modulus, for example, `result = num1 % num2;`
	++	Incremental operator that increases the value by 1. , for example, `var result = num1++;`
	--	Decrement operator that decreases the value by 1, for example, `var result = num1--;`
Relational operators	==	Determines whether the two operands are of the same value. It returns True if the expression is successful; otherwise it returns false, for example, `var result = num1 == num2;`

	!=	Performs the same as == but negates the comparison; if two operands are equal, it returns false, for example, `var result = num1 != num2;`
	>	Determines whether in expression, the left operand is greater than the right operand and returns True on success, for example, `var result = num1 > num2;`
	<	Determines whether in expression, the left operand is less than the right operand and returns true on success, for example, `var result = num1 < num2;`
	>=	Determines whether in expression, the value of the left operand is greater than or equal to the value of the right operand and returns true on success, for example, `var result = num1 <= num2;`
	<=	Determines whether in expression, the value of the left operand is less than or equal to the value of the right operand and returns true on success, for example, `var result = num1 <= num2;`
Logical operators	&&	This is a logical AND operator. Expression evaluates on the basis of the left operand; if it's true, then the right operand would not be ignored, for example, `var result = num1 && num2;`
	||	This is a logical OR operator. Expression evaluates to true if any of the operands is true, for example, `var result = num1 || num2;`
	!	This is called the logical NOT operator. It reverses the evaluation result, for example, `var result = !(num1 && num2);`
Bitwise operators	|	This is a bitwise OR operator and works on bits. If either of the bits is 1, the result will be 1, for example, `var result = num1 | num2;`
	&	This is a bitwise AND operator and works on bits. If either of the bits is 0, then the result is 0; otherwise, it's 1, for example, `var result = num1 & num2;`
	^	This is a bitwise XOR operator and works on bits. If bits are the same, the result is 0; otherwise, it's 1, for example, `var result = num1 ^ num2;`

	~	This is a unary operator and is called a bitwise COMPLEMENT operator. This works on a single operand and reverses the bit, which means if the bit is 0, then it returns 1 and vice- versa, for example, `var result = ~num1;`
	<<	This is a bitwise left shift operator and shifts a number to the left by the number of bits specified in the expression and adds the zeros to the least significant bits, for example, `var result = num1 << 1;`
	>>	This is a bitwise right shift operator and shifts a number to the right by the number of bits specified in the expression, for example, `var result = num1 >> 1;`
Assignment operators	=	The assignment operator that assigns values from right-hand side to the left-hand side operand, for example, `var result = nim1 + num2;`
	+=	The add and assign operator; It adds and assigns values of the right operands to the left operands, for example, `result += num1;`
	-=	The subtract and assign operator; It subtracts and assigns values of the right operands to the left operands, for example, `result -= num1;`
	*=	The multiply and assign operator; It multiplies and assigns values of the right operands to the left operands, for example, `result *= num1;`
	/=	The divide and assign operator; It divides and assigns values of the right operands to the left operands, for example, `result /= num1;`
	%=	The modulus and assign operator; It takes modulus of the left and right operands and assigns value to the left operands, for example, `result %= num1;`
	<<=	Bitwise left shifts and assignment, for example, `result <<= 2;`
	>>;=	Bitwise right shifts and assignment, for example, `result >>= 2;`
	&=	Bitwise AND and assignment operator, for example,. `result &= Num1;`

	^=	Bitwise XOR and assignment operator, for example, result ^= num1;
.	|=	Bitwise OR and assignment operator, for example, result |= num1;

Take a look at the following code snippet, which implements all operators discussed previously:

```
private void ArithmeticOperators()
{
WriteLine("\nArithmetic operators\n");
WriteLine($"Operator '+' (add): {nameof(Num1)} + {nameof(Num2)} = {Num1 +
Num2}");
WriteLine($"Operator '-' (substract): {nameof(Num1)} - {nameof(Num2)} =
{Num1 - Num2}");
WriteLine($"Operator '*' (multiplication): {nameof(Num1)} * {nameof(Num2)}
= {Num1 * Num2}");
WriteLine($"Operator '/' (division): {nameof(Num1)} / {nameof(Num2)} =
{Num1 / Num2}");
WriteLine($"Operator '%' (modulus): {nameof(Num1)} % {nameof(Num2)} = {Num1
% Num2}");
WriteLine($"Operator '++' (incremental): pre-increment: ++{nameof(Num1)} =
{++Num1}");
WriteLine($"Operator '++' (incremental): post-increment: {nameof(Num1)}++ =
{Num1++}");
WriteLine($"Operator '--' (decremental): pre-decrement: --{nameof(Num2)} =
{--Num2}");
WriteLine($"Operator '--' (decremental): post-decrement: {nameof(Num2)}-- =
{Num2--}");
ReadLine();
}
//Code omitted
```

The complete code is available on the GitHub repository, and it produces the following results:

```
Operators example

Enter first number:58
Enter second number:15_

Num1=58
Num2=15


Arithmetic operators

Operator '+' (add): Num1 + Num2 = 73
Operator '-' (substract): Num1 - Num2 = 43
Operator '*' (multiplication): Num1 * Num2 = 870
Operator '/' (division): Num1 / Num2 = 3
Operator '%' (modulus): Num1 % Num2 = 13
Operator '++' (incremental): pre-increment: ++Num1 = 59
Operator '++' (incremental): post-increment: Num1++ = 59
Operator '--' (decremental): pre-decrement: --Num2 = 14
Operator '--' (decremental): post-decrement: Num2-- = 14


Relational operators

Operator '==' (equal): Num1 == Num2 = False
Operator '!=' (not equal): Num1 != Num2 = True
Operator '>' (greater than): Num1 > Num2 = True
Operator '<' (less than): Num1 < Num2 = False
Operator '>=' (greater than or equal): Num1 >= Num2 = True
Operator '<=' (less than or equal): Num1 <= Num2 = False
Logical operators

bln1 = False
bln2 = True

Operator '&&' (AND): bln1 && bln2 = False
Operator '||' (OR): bln1 || bln2 = True
Operator '!' (NOT): bln1 ! bln2 = True


Bitwise operators

Binary of 60 = 00111100
Binary of 13 = 00001101

Operator '|' (OR): Num1 | Num2 = 61
In Binary: 00111100 | 00001101 = 00111101
Operator '&' (AND): Num1 & Num2 = 12
In Binary: 00111100 & 00001101 = 00001100
Operator '^' (XOR): Num1 ^ Num2 = 49
In Binary: 00111100 ^ 00001101 = 00110001
Operator '~' (COMPLEMENT): ~Num1 = -61
In Binary: ~00111100 = 11111111111111111111111111000011
Operator '~' (COMPLEMENT): ~Num2 = -14
In Binary: ~00001101 = 11111111111111111111111111110010
Operator '<<' (Shift Left): Num1<<1 = 120
In Binary: 00111100<<1 = 01111000
Operator '>>' (Shift Right): Num1>>1 = 30
In Binary: 00111100>>1 = 00011110


Assignment operators

Operator '=' (assignmnet): result=Num1 + Num2 where result contains value: 73
Operator '+=' (add and assign): result+=Num1 where result contains value: 60
Operator '-=' (substrcat and assign): result-=Num1 where result contains value: 0
Operator '*=' (multiply and assign): result*=Num1 where result contains value: 0
Operator '/=' (divide and assign): result/=Num1 where result contains value: 0
Operator '%=' (modulus and assign): result%=Num1 where result contains value: 0
```

Discussing operator precedence in C#

The calculation or evaluation of any expression and the order of operators is very important. This is what is called operator precedence. We have all read the mathematic rule *Order of Operator*, which is abbreviated as *BODMAS*. Refer to https://www.skillsyouneed. com/num/bodmas.html to refresh your memory. So, mathematics teaches us how to solve an expression; in a similar way, our C# should follow rules to solve or evaluate the expression. For instance, *3+2*5* evaluates as *13* and not *25*. So, in this equation, the rule is to first multiply and then add. That's why it evaluates as *2*5 = 10* and then *3+10 = 13*. You can set a higher precedence order by applying braces, so if you do this in the preceding statement *(3+2)*5*, it results in *25*.

 To know more about operator precedence, refer to https://msdn. microsoft.com/en-us/library/aa691323(VS.71).aspx.

This is a simple code snippet to evaluate the expression:

```
private void OperatorPrecedence()
{
Write("Enter first number:");
    Num1 = Convert.ToInt32(ReadLine());
Write("Enter second number:");
    Num2 = Convert.ToInt32(ReadLine());
Write("Enter third number:");
    Num3 = Convert.ToInt32(ReadLine());
Write("Enter fourth number:");
    Num4 = Convert.ToInt32(ReadLine());
int result = Num1 + Num2 * Num3/Num4;
WriteLine($"Num1 + Num2 * Num3/Num4 = {result}");
    result = Num1 + Num2 * (Num3 / Num4);
WriteLine($"Num1 + Num2 * (Num3/Num4) = {result}");
    result = (Num1 + (Num2 * Num3)) / Num4;
WriteLine($"(Num1 + (Num2 * Num3)) /Num4 = {result}");
    result = (Num1 + Num2) * Num3 / Num4;
WriteLine($"(Num1 + Num2) * Num3/Num4 = {result}");
ReadLine();
}
```

The preceding code produces the following results:

```
Enter first number:15
Enter second number:10
Enter third number:8
Enter fourth number:15
Num1 + Num2 * Num3/Num4 = 20
Num1 + Num2 * (Num3/Num4) = 15
(Num1 + (Num2 * Num3)) /Num4 = 6
(Num1 + Num2) * Num3/Num4 = 13
```

Operator overloading

Operator loading is a way to redefine the actual functionality of a particular operator. This is important when you're working with user-defined complex types, where the direct use of in-built operators is impossible. For instance, say, you have an object with numerous properties and you want an addition of two for these types of objects. It is not possible like this: `VeryComplexObject = result = verycoplexobj1 + verycomplexobj2;`. To overcome such a situation, overloading does the magic.

 You cannot overload all inbuilt operators; refer to `https://docs.microsoft.com/en-us/dotnet/csharp/programming-guide/statements-expressions-operators/overloadable-operators` to see what operators are overloadable.

Let's consider the following code snippet to see how operator loading works (note that this code is not complete; refer to Github for the complete source code):

```
public struct Coordinate
{
//code omitted

public static Coordinateoperator +(Coordinate coordinate1, Coordinate
coordinate2) =>;
new Coordinate(coordinate1._xAxis + coordinate2._xAxis, coordinate1._yAxis
+ coordinate2._yAxis);
public static Coordinateoperator-(Coordinate coordinate1, Coordinate
coordinate2) =>
new Coordinate(coordinate1._xAxis - coordinate2._xAxis, coordinate1._yAxis
- coordinate2._yAxis);
public static Coordinateoperator *(Coordinate coordinate1, Coordinate
coordinate2) =>
new Coordinate(coordinate1._xAxis * coordinate2._xAxis, coordinate1._yAxis
```

```
* coordinate2._yAxis);
//code omitted

public static booloperator ==(Coordinate coordinate1, Coordinate
coordinate2) =>;
        coordinate1._xAxis == coordinate2._xAxis && coordinate1._yAxis ==
coordinate2._yAxis;

public static booloperator !=(Coordinate coordinate1, Coordinate
coordinate2) => !(coordinate1 == coordinate2);

//code omitted

public double Area() => _xAxis * _yAxis;

public override string ToString() =>$"({_xAxis},{_yAxis})";
}
```

In the preceding code, we have a new type coordinate, which is a surface of *x* axis and *y* axis. Now if we want to apply some operations, that is not possible with the use of inbuilt operators. With the help of operator overloading, we enhance the actual functionality of inbuilt operators. The following code is the consumed coordinate type:

```
private static void OperatorOverloadigExample()
{
WriteLine("Operator overloading example\n");
Write("Enter x-axis of Surface1: ");
var x1 = ReadLine();
Write("Enter y-axis of Surface1: ");
var y1 = ReadLine();
Write("Enter x-axis of Surface2: ");
var x2= ReadLine();
Write("Enter y-axis of Surface2: ");
var y2= ReadLine();

var surface1 = new Coordinate(Convert.ToInt32(x1),Convert.ToInt32(y1));
var surface2 = new Coordinate(Convert.ToInt32(x2),Convert.ToInt32(y2));
WriteLine();
Clear();
WriteLine($"Surface1:{surface1}");
WriteLine($"Area of Surface1:{surface1.Area()}");
WriteLine($"Surface2:{surface2}");
WriteLine($"Area of Surface2:{surface2.Area()}");
WriteLine();
WriteLine($"surface1 == surface2: {surface1==surface2}");
WriteLine($"surface1 < surface2: {surface1 < surface2}");
WriteLine($"surface1 > surface2: {surface1 > surface2}");
WriteLine($"surface1 <= surface2: {surface1 <= surface2}");
```

```
WriteLine($"surface1 >= surface2: {surface1 >= surface2}");
WriteLine();
var surface3 = surface1 + surface2;
WriteLine($"Addition: {nameof(surface1)} + {nameof(surface2)} =
{surface3}");
WriteLine($"{nameof(surface3)}:{surface3}");
WriteLine($"Area of {nameof(surface3)}: {surface3.Area()} ");
WriteLine();
WriteLine($"Substraction: {nameof(surface1)} - {nameof(surface2)} =
{surface1-surface2}");
WriteLine($"Multiplication: {nameof(surface1)} * {nameof(surface2)} =
{surface1 * surface2}");
WriteLine($"Division: {nameof(surface1)} / {nameof(surface2)} = {surface1 /
surface2}");
WriteLine($"Modulus: {nameof(surface1)} % {nameof(surface2)} = {surface1 %
surface2}");
}
```

In the preceding code snippet, we declared a variable of our struct *Coordinate* and call operators for various operations. Note that by overloading, we have changed the actual behavior of the operator, for instance, the add (+) operator, which generally adds two numbers, but with the implementation here, the add (+) operator gives the sum of two surfaces. The complete code produces the following result:

```
Surface1:(4,5)
Area of Surface1:20
Surface2:(2,9)
Area of Surface2:18

surface1 == surface2: False
surface1 < surface2: False
surface1 > surface2: False
surface1 <= surface2: False
surface1 >= surface2: False

Addition: surface1 + surface2 = (6,14)
surface3:(6,14)
Area of surface3: 84

Substraction: surface1 - surface2 = (2,-4)
Multiplication: surface1 * surface2 = (8,45)
Division: surface1 / surface2 = (2,0)
Modulus: surface1 % surface2 = (0,5)
```

An overview of type conversion

Type conversion means converting one type into another type. Alternatively, we call it as casting or type casting. Type conversion is broadly divided into the following categories.

Implicit conversion

Implicit conversion is the conversion that is performed by the C# compiler internally to match the the type of variable by assignment of values to that variable. This action happens implicitly, and there's no need to write any extra code to obey the type-safe mechanism. In implicit conversions, only smaller to larger types and derived classes to base class is possible.

Explicit conversion

Explicit conversion is the conversion that is performed by the user explicitly with the use of the cast operator; that's why this is also known as type casting. Explicit conversion is also possible using built-in type conversion methods. For more information, refer to https:// docs.microsoft.com/en-us/dotnet/csharp/language-reference/keywords/explicit- numeric-conversions-table.

Let's take a look at the following code snippet, which shows implicit/explicit type conversion in action:

```
private static void ImplicitExplicitTypeConversionExample()
{
WriteLine("Implicit conversion");
int numberInt = 2589;
double doubleNumber = numberInt; // implicit type conversion

WriteLine($"{nameof(numberInt)} of type:{numberInt.GetType().FullName} has
value:{numberInt}");
WriteLine($"{nameof(doubleNumber)} of
type:{doubleNumber.GetType().FullName} implicitly type casted and has
value:{doubleNumber}");

WriteLine("Implicit conversion");
doubleNumber = 2589.05D;
numberInt = (int)doubleNumber; //explicit type conversion
WriteLine($"{nameof(doubleNumber)} of
type:{doubleNumber.GetType().FullName} has value:{doubleNumber}");
WriteLine($"{nameof(numberInt)} of type:{numberInt.GetType().FullName}
```

```
explicitly type casted and has value:{numberInt}");
}
```

In the preceding code-snippet, we discussed implicit and explicit conversion when we assign a variable `numberInt` of int type to a variable `doubleNumber` of double type, which is called implicit type conversion, and the reverse is an explicit type conversion that requires a casting using int. Note that implicitly, type conversion does not require any casting, but explicitly, conversion requires type casting, and there are chances for loss of data during explicit conversion. For instance, our explicit conversion from double to int would result in a loss of data (all precision would be truncated while a value is assigned to int type variable). This code produces the following result:

```
Day02 - Learn C# in 7-days
Implicit conversion
numberInt of type:System.Int32 has value:2589
doubleNumber of type:System.Double implicitly type casted and has value:2589
Implicit conversion
doubleNumber of type:System.Double has value:2589.05
numberInt of type:System.Int32 explicitly type casted and has value:2589
```

The two most important language fundamentals are type conversion and casting. To know more about these two, refer to `https://docs.microsoft.com/en-us/dotnet/csharp/programming-guide/types/casting-and-type-conversions`.

Understanding statements

In C#, you can evaluate different kinds of expression that would or would not generate the results. Whenever you say something like *what would happen if result >0*, in that case, we are stating something. This can be a decision-making statement, result-making statement, assignment statement, or any other activity statement. On the other hand, loops are a code block that repeatedly executes a couple of statements.

In this section, we will discuss statements and loops in detail.

A statement should perform some action before returning a result. In other words, if you are writing a statement, that statement should say something. To do that, it has to execute some inbuilt or custom operations. Statements can depend upon a decision or can be a part of the result of any existing statement. The official page (https://docs.microsoft.com/en-us/dotnet/csharp/programming-guide/statements-expressions-operators/statements) defines statement as:

> *A statement can consist of a single line of code that ends in a semicolon, or a series of single-line statements in a block. A statement block is enclosed in {} brackets and can contain nested blocks.*

Take a look at the following code snippet, which shows different statements:

```
private static void StatementExample()
{
WriteLine("Statement example:");
int singleLineStatement; //declarative statement
WriteLine("'intsingleLineStatement;' is a declarative statment.");
singleLineStatement = 125; //assignment statement
WriteLine("'singleLineStatement = 125;' is an assignmnet statement.");
WriteLine($"{nameof(singleLineStatement)} = {singleLineStatement}");
var persons = newList<Person>
    {
     newAuthor {Name = "Gaurav Aroraa" }
    }; //declarative and assignmnet statement
WriteLine("'var persons = new List&lt;Person&gt;();' is a declarative and
assignmnet statement.");

//block statement
foreach (var person in persons)
    {
     WriteLine("'foreach (var person in persons){}' is a block
statement.");
     WriteLine($"Name:{person.Name}");
    }
}
```

In the preceding code, we used three type statements: declarative, assignment, and block statements. The code produces the following result:

```
Day02 - Learn C# in 7-days
Statement example:
'int singleLineStatement;' is a declarative statment.
'singleLineStatement = 125;' is an assignmnet statement.
singleLineStatement = 125
'var persons = new List<Person>();' is a declarative and assignmnet statement.
'foreach (var person in persons){}' is a block statement.
Name:Gaurav Aroraa
```

According to the official page (https://docs.microsoft.com/en-us/dotnet/csharp/programming-guide/statements-expressions-operators/statements), C# statements can be broadly divided into the following categories.

Declarative statement

Whenever you declare a variable or constant, you are writing a declarative statement. You can also assign the values to variables at the time of declaration of variables. Assigning values to variables at time of declaration is an optional task, but constants are required to assign values at the time you declared them.

This is a typical declarative statement:

```
int singleLineStatement; //declarative statement
```

Expression statement

In an expression statement, the expression that is on the right-hand side evaluates results and assigns that result to the left-hand side variable. An expression statement could be an assignment, method invocation, or new object creation. This is the typical expression statement example:

```
Console.WriteLine($"Member name:{Name}");
var result = Num1 + Num2 * Num3 / Num4;
```

Selection statement

This is also called a decision-making statement. Statements are branched as per the condition and their evaluations. The condition may be one or more than one. The selection or decision statement falls under if...else, and switch case. In this section, we will discuss these statements in detail.

The if statement

The if statement is a decision statement that could branch one or more statements to evaluate. This statement consists of a Boolean expression. Let's consider the problem of finding vowels in a book that was discussed on day one. Let's write this using the if statement:

```
private static void IfStatementExample()
{
WriteLine("if statement example.");
Write("Enter character:");
char inputChar = Convert.ToChar(ReadLine());

//so many if statement, compiler go through all if statement
//not recommended way
if (char.ToLower(inputChar) == 'a')
WriteLine($"Character {inputChar} is a vowel.");
if (char.ToLower(inputChar) == 'e')
WriteLine($"Character {inputChar} is a vowel.");
if (char.ToLower(inputChar) == 'i')
WriteLine($"Character {inputChar} is a vowel.");
if (char.ToLower(inputChar) == 'o')
WriteLine($"Character {inputChar} is a vowel.");
if (char.ToLower(inputChar) == 'u')
WriteLine($"Character {inputChar} is a vowel.");
}
```

In the preceding code, we are using only the `if` condition. However, the preceding code is not a recommended code, but this is just there to showcase the usage of the `if` statement. In the preceding code snippet, once the code executes a compiler, it verifies all `if` statements without caring about the scenario where my first `if` statement got passed. Say, if you enter *a*, which is a vowel in this case, the compiler finds the first expression to be true and prints the output (we get our result), then the compiler checks the next `if` statement, and so on. In this case, the compiler unnecessarily checks the rest of all four statements that should not have happened. There might be a scenario where our code does not fall into any of the `if` statements in the preceding code; in that case, we would not get the expected result. To overcome such situations, we have the `if...else` statement, which we are going to discuss in the upcoming section.

The if..else statement

In this `if` statement followed by else and the else block execute in case evaluation of if block is false. This is a simple example:

```
private static void IfElseStatementExample()
{
WriteLine("if statement example.");
Write("Enter character:");
char inputChar = Convert.ToChar(ReadLine());
char[] vowels = {'a', 'e', 'i', 'o', 'u'};

if (vowels.Contains(char.ToLower(inputChar)))
WriteLine($"Character '{inputChar}' is a vowel.");
else
WriteLine($"Character '{inputChar}' is a consonent.");
}
```

In the preceding code snippet, we are using `else` followed by the `if` statement. When the `if` statement evaluates to false, then the `else` block code will be executed.

if...else if...else statement

The `if...else` statement is very important when you need to test multiple conditions. In this statement, the `if` statement evaluates first, then the `else if` statement, and at last the else block executes. Here, the `if` statement may or may not have the `if...else` statement or block; `if...else` always comes after the `if` block and before the `else` block. The `else` statement is the final code block in the `if...else...if else...else` statement, which indicates that none of preceding conditions evaluate to true.

Take a look at the following code snippet:

```
private static void IfElseIfElseStatementExample()
{
WriteLine("if statement example.");
Write("Enter character:");
char inputChar = Convert.ToChar(ReadLine());

if (char.ToLower(inputChar) == 'a')
{ WriteLine($"Character {inputChar} is a vowel."); }
elseif (char.ToLower(inputChar) == 'e')
{ WriteLine($"Character {inputChar} is a vowel."); }
elseif (char.ToLower(inputChar) == 'i')
{ WriteLine($"Character {inputChar} is a vowel."); }
elseif (char.ToLower(inputChar) == 'o')
{ WriteLine($"Character {inputChar} is a vowel."); }
elseif (char.ToLower(inputChar) == 'u')
{ WriteLine($"Character {inputChar} is a vowel."); }
else
{ WriteLine($"Character '{inputChar}' is a consonant."); }
}
```

In the preceding code snippet, we have various `if...else if...else` statements that evaluate the expression: whether `inputchar` is equivalent to comparative `characternot`. In this code, if you enter a character other than *a,e,i,o,u* that does not fall in any of the preceding condition, then the case `else` code block executes and it produces the final result. So, when `else` executes, it returns the result by saying that the entered character is a consonant.

Nested if statement

Nested `if` statements are nothing but `if` statement blocks within `if` statement blocks. Similarly, we can nest `else` `if` statement blocks. This is a simple code snippet:

```
private static void NestedIfStatementExample()
{
WriteLine("nested if statement example.");
Write("Enter your age:");
int age = Convert.ToInt32(ReadLine());

if (age < 18)
    {
      WriteLine("Your age should be equal or greater than 18yrs.");
      if (age < 15)
        {
         WriteLine("You need to complete your school first");
```

```
        }
    }
}
```

Switch statement

This is a statement that provides a way to select an expression using `switch` statement that evaluates the conditions using `case` blocks when code does not fall in any of the `case` blocks; then, the `default` block executes (default block is an optional block in `switch...case` statement).

Switch statement is also known as an alternative to `if...else if...else` statement. Let's rewrite our examples used in the previous section to showcase the `if...else if...else` statement:

```
private static void SwitchCaseExample()
{
WriteLine("switch case statement example.");
Write("Enter character:");
charinputChar = Convert.ToChar(ReadLine());

switch (char.ToLower(inputChar))
{
case'a':
WriteLine($"Character {inputChar} is a vowel.");
break;
case'e':
WriteLine($"Character {inputChar} is a vowel.");
break;
case'i':
WriteLine($"Character {inputChar} is a vowel.");
break;
case'o':
WriteLine($"Character {inputChar} is a vowel.");
break;
case'u':
WriteLine($"Character {inputChar} is a vowel.");
break;
default:
WriteLine($"Character '{inputChar}' is a consonant.");
break;
}
}
```

In the preceding code, the default block will execute if none of the case evaluates to true. The `switch...case` statement will be discussed in detail on day three.

There is a slight difference when you're choosing between `switch...case` and `if...else`. Refer to `https://stackoverflow.com/questions/94305/what-is-quicker-switch-on-string-or-elseif-on-type` for more details.

Iteration statement

These statements provide a way to iterate collection data. There may be a case where you want to execute a code block multiple times or a repetitive action is required on the same activity. There are iteration loops available to achieve this. Code blocks within the loop statement execute sequentially, which means the first statement executes first, and so on. The following are the main categories into which we can divide iteration statements of C#:

The do...while loop

This helps us execute a statement or a statement of block repeatedly until it evaluates the expression to false. In `do...while` statement, a block of statement executes first and then it checks the condition under `while`, which means a statement or block of statements that execute at least once.

Take a look at the following code:

```
private static void DoWhileStatementExample()
{
WriteLine("do...while example");
Write("Enter repeatitive length:");
int length = Convert.ToInt32(ReadLine());
int count = 0;
do
    {
        count++;
        WriteLine(newstring('*',count));
    } while (count < length);
}
```

In the preceding code snippet, the statement of the `do` block executes until the statement of the while block evaluates to false.

The while loop

This executes the statement or code block until the condition evaluates to true. In this expression evaluates before the execution of code-block, if expression evaluates to false, loop terminates and no statement or code-block execute. Take a look at the following code snippet:

```
private static void WhileStatementExample()
{
WriteLine("while example");
Write("Enter repeatitive length:");
int length = Convert.ToInt32(ReadLine());
int count = 0;
while (count < length)
    {
        count++;
        WriteLine(newstring('*', count));
    }
}
```

The preceding code executes the while statement repeatedly until expression evaluates to false.

The for loop

The for loop is similar to other loops that help run a statement or code block repeatedly until an expression evaluates to false. The for loop takes three sections: the initializer, condition, and iterator, where the initializer section executes first and only once; this is nothing but a variable to start a loop. The next section is condition, and if it evaluates to true, then only body statements are executed; otherwise it terminates the loop. The third and most important section is incremental or iterator, which updates the loop control variable. Let's take a look at the following code snippet:

```
private static void ForStatementExample()
{
WriteLine("for loop example.");
Write("Enter repeatitive length:");
int length = Convert.ToInt32(ReadLine());
for (intcountIndex = 0; countIndex < length; countIndex++)
    {
     WriteLine(newstring('*', countIndex));
    }
}
```

The preceding code snippet is a working example of a `for` loop. Here, our code statement within the `for` loop block will executive repeatedly until the `countIndex&lt; length` expression evaluates to false.

The foreach loop

This helps iterate an array element or collection. It does the same thing as the `for` loop, but this is available to iterate through a collection without the facility to add or remove items from collections.

Let's take a look at the following code snippet:

```
private static void ForEachStatementExample()
{
WriteLine("foreach loop example");
char[] vowels = {'a', 'e', 'i', 'o', 'u'};
WriteLine("foreach on Array.");
foreach (var vowel in vowels)
    {
        WriteLine($"{vowel}");
    }
WriteLine();
var persons = new List<Person>
    {
    new Author {Name = "Gaurav Aroraa"},
    new Reviewer {Name = "ShivprasadKoirala"},
    new TeamMember {Name = "Vikas Tiwari"},
    new TeamMember {Name = "Denim Pinto"}
    };
WriteLine("foreach on collection");
foreach (var person in persons)
    {
        WriteLine($"{person.Name}");
    }
}
```

The preceding code is a working example of a `foreach` statement that prints a person's name. `Name` is a property in a collection of the `Person` object. The statement of the `foreach` block executes repeatedly until the expression `person in persons` evaluates to false.

The jump statement

The jump statement, as is self-explanatory from the name, is a statement that helps move control from one section to another. These are the main jump statements in C#.

break

This terminates the control flow `for` loop or in `switch` statement. Take a look at the following example:

```
private static void BreakStatementExample()
{
WriteLine("break statement example");
WriteLine("break in for loop");
for (int count = 0; count &lt; 50; count++
{
if (count == 8)
    {
     break;
    }
WriteLine($"{count}");
}
WriteLine();
WriteLine("break in switch statement");
SwitchCaseExample();
}
```

In the preceding code, execution of the `for` loop will break as soon as the `if` expression evaluates to true.

continue

This helps `continue` the control to the next iteration of loop, and it comes with `while`, `do`, `for`, or `foreach` loops. Take a look at the following example:

```
private static void ContinueStatementExample()
{
WriteLine("continue statement example");
WriteLine("continue in for loop");
for (int count = 0; count &lt; 15; count++)
```

```
{
if (count< 8)
{
 continue;
}
 WriteLine($"{count}");
}
}
```

The preceding code bypasses the execution when the `if` expression evaluates to true.

default

This comes with a `switch` statement and a `default` block that makes sure that `if` no match found in any of the `case` blocks, the `default` block executes. Refer to the `switch...case` statement for more detail.

Exception-handling statement

This has the ability to handle unknown issues within a program, which is known as exceptional handling (we will discuss exception handling on day four).

Arrays and string manipulations

Arrays and strings are important in C# programming. There may be chances when you need string manipulation or play with complex data using arrays. In this section, we will discuss arrays and strings.

Arrays

An array is nothing but a data structure that stores fixed-size sequential elements of the same type. Elements of an array that contained data are basically variables, and we can also call an array a collection of variables of the same type, and this type is generally called an element type.

An array is a block of contiguous memory. This block stores everything required for an array, that is, elements, element rank, and length of the array. The first element rank is 0 and the last element rank is equal to the total length of array - 1.

Let's consider the `char[] vowels = {'a', 'e', 'i', 'o', 'u'};` array. An array with size five. Every element is stored in a sequential manner and can be accessed using its element rank. The following is the diagram showing what things an array declaration contains:

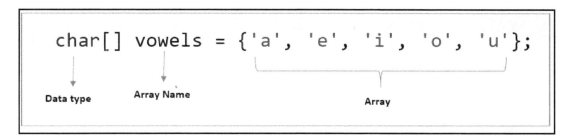

The preceding figure is a representation of our array declaration for vowels that are of *Data type* char. Here, *[ ]* represents an array and tells CLR that we are declaring an array of characters. Vowels is a variable name and the right-hand side representation of a complete array that contains data.

The following figure depicts what this array looks like in memory:

vowels[0]	vowels[1]	vowels[2]	vowels[3]	vowels[4]

In the preceding figure, we have a group of contiguous memory blocks. This also tells us that the lowest address of an array in memory corresponds to the first element of an array and the highest address of the array in memory corresponds to the last element.

We can retrieve the value of an element by its rank (starting with 0). So, in the preceding code, *vowels[0]* will give us *a* and *vowels[4]* will give us *u*.

 When we talk about an array, we mean a reference type because array types are reference types. Array types are derived from `System.Array`, which is a class. Hence, all array types are reference types.

Alternatively, we can also get the values using `for`, which iterates until the `rankIndex <` `vowels.Length` expression evaluates to false and the code block of the `for` loop statement prints the array element based on its rank:

```
private static void ArrayExample()
{
WriteLine("Array example.\n");
char[] vowels = {'a', 'e', 'i', 'o', 'u'};
WriteLine("char[] vowels = {'a', 'e', 'i', 'o', 'u'};\n");
WriteLine("acces array using for loop");
for (intrankIndex = 0; rankIndex&lt;vowels.Length; rankIndex++)
{
    Write($"{vowels[rankIndex]} ");
}
WriteLine();
WriteLine("acces array using foreach loop");
foreach (char vowel in vowels)
    {
        Write($"{vowel} ");
    }
}
```

The preceding code produces the following results:

```
Day02 - Learn C# in 7-days
Array example.

char[] vowels = {'a', 'e', 'i', 'o', 'u'};

acces array using for loop
a e i o u
acces array using foreach loop
a e i o u
```

In the preceding example, we initialized the array and assigned data to a statement that is equivalent to `char[] vowels = newchar[5];`. Here, we are telling CLR that we are creating an array named vowels of type char that has a maximum of five elements. Alternatively, we can also declare the same `char[] vowels = newchar[5] { 'a', 'e', 'i', 'o', 'u' };`

In this section, we will discuss the different types of arrays and see how we can use arrays in different scenarios.

Types of arrays

Earlier, we discussed what an array is and how we can declare an array. Until now, we have discussed an array of single dimension. Consider a matrix where we have rows and columns. Arrays are a representation of data arranged in rows and columns in respect of the matrix. However, arrays have more types as discussed here.

Single-dimensional array

A single-dimensional array can be declared simply by initializing the array class and setting up the size. Here is a single-dimensional array:

```
string[] cardinalDirections = {"North","East","South","West"};
```

Multidimensional array

Arrays can be declared as more than one-dimension, which that means you can create a matrix of rows and columns. Multidimensional arrays could be two-dimensional arrays, three-dimensional arrays, or more. Different ways to create a typical two-dimensional array of 2x2 size means two rows and two columns:

```
int[,] numbers = new int[2,2];
int[,] numbers = new int[2, 2] {{1,2},{3,4} };
```

Following is the code-snippet that accesses the two-dimensional array:

```
int[,] numbers = new int[2, 2] {{1,2},{3,4} };
for (introwsIndex = 0; rowsIndex< 2; rowsIndex++)
{
for (intcolIndex = 0; colIndex< 2; colIndex++)
    {
        WriteLine($"numbers[{rowsIndex},{colIndex}] = {numbers[rowsIndex,
colIndex]}");
    }
}
```

The preceding code snippet is a representation of an array of 2x2, that is, two rows and two columns. In mathematical terms, we also know this as a square matrix. To retrieve the elements of this array, we need at least two `for` loops; the outer loop will work on rows and the inner loop will work on columns, and finally, we can get the element value using `number[rowIndex][colIndex]`.

A square matrix is the one with the same rows and columns. Generally, it is called an *n* by *n* matrix.

This code produces the following results:

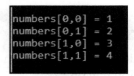

```
numbers[0,0] = 1
numbers[0,1] = 2
numbers[1,0] = 3
numbers[1,1] = 4
```

Jagged array

Jagged array is an array of array or array in array. In a jagged array, the element of array is an array. You can also set an array's element with different sizes/dimensions. Any element of jagged array can have another array.

A typical declaration of a jagged array is as follows:

```
string[][,] collaborators = new string[5][,];
```

Consider the following code-snippet:

```
WriteLine("Jagged array.\n");
string[][,] collaborators = new string[3][,]
{
new[,] {{"Name", "ShivprasadKoirala"}, {"Age", "40"}},
new[,] {{"Name", "Gaurav Aroraa" }, {"Age", "43"}},
new[,] {{"Name", "Vikas Tiwari"}, {"Age", "28"}}
};

for (int index = 0; index <collaborators.Length; index++)
{
    for (introwIndex = 0; rowIndex< 2; rowIndex++)
    {
        for (intcolIndex = 0; colIndex< 2; colIndex++)
        {
            WriteLine($"collaborators[{index}][{rowIndex},
            {colIndex}] = {collaborators[index]
            [rowIndex,colIndex]}");
        }
    }
}
```

In the preceding code, we are declaring a jagged array of three elements that contain a two-dimensional array. After execution, it produces the following results:

```
Jagged array.

collaborators[0][0,0] = Name
collaborators[0][0,1] = Shivprasad Koirala
collaborators[0][1,0] = Age
collaborators[0][1,1] = 40
collaborators[1][0,0] = Name
collaborators[1][0,1] = Gaurav Aroraa
collaborators[1][1,0] = Age
collaborators[1][1,1] = 43
collaborators[2][0,0] = Name
collaborators[2][0,1] = Vikas Tiwari
collaborators[2][1,0] = Age
collaborators[2][1,1] = 28
```

You can also declare more complex arrays to interact with more complex scenarios. You can get more information by referring to https://docs.microsoft.com/en-us/dotnet/api/system.array?view=netcore-2.0.

Implicitly typed arrays can be created as well. In implicitly typed arrays, the array type inferred from the elements is defined during array initialization, for instance, var charArray = new[] {'a', 'e', 'i', 'o', 'u'}; here we declare a char array. For more information on implicitly typed arrays, refer to https://docs.microsoft.com/en-us/dotnet/csharp/programming-guide/arrays/implicitly-typed-arrays.

Strings

In C#, a string is nothing but an array of characters that represents UTF-16 code units and is used to represent a text.

The maximum size of a string in memory is 2 GB.

The declaration of a string object is as simple as you declaring any variable the most commonly used statement: string authorName = "Gaurav Aroraa";.

A string object is called immutable, which means it is read-only. A string object's value cannot be modified after it is created. Every operation that you perform on a string object returns a new string. As strings are immutable, they cause a huge performance penalty because every operation on a string needs to create a new string. To overcome this, the `StringBuilder` object is available in the `System.Text` class.

 For more information on strings, refer to `https://docs.microsoft.com/en-us/dotnet/api/system.string?view=netcore-2.0#Immutability`.

These are the alternative ways to declare string objects:

```
private static void StringExample()
{
WriteLine("String object creation");
string authorName = "Gaurav Aroraa"; //string literal assignment
WriteLine($"{authorName}");
string property = "Name: ";
string person = "Gaurav";
string personName = property + person; //string concatenation
WriteLine($"{personName}");

char[] language = {'c', 's', 'h', 'a', 'r', 'p'};
stringstr Language = new string(language); //initializing the constructor
WriteLine($"{strLanguage}");
string repeatMe = new string('*', 5);
WriteLine($"{repeatMe}");
string[] members = {"Shivprasad", "Denim", "Vikas", "Gaurav"};
string name = string.Join(" ", members);
WriteLine($"{name}");
}
```

The preceding code snippets tells us that the declaration can be done as follows:

- String literal assignment while declaring a string variable
- While concatenating string
- Constructor initialization using `new`
- Method returning string

 There are plenty of string methods and formatting actions that are available for string operations; refer to `https://docs.microsoft.com/en-us/dotnet/api/system.string?view=netcore-2.0` for more details.

Structure versus class

Similar to a class in C#, a struct is also a data structure that consists of members, functions, and so on. Classes are reference types, but structs are value types; hence, these are not required for heap allocation but for allocation on the stack.

Value type data will be allocated on stack and reference type data will be allocated on heap. A value type that is used in struct is stored on the stack, but when the same value type is used in an array, it is stored in a heap.

 For more details on heap and stack memory allocation, refer to `http://www-ee.eng.hawaii.edu/~tep/EE160/Book/chap14/subsection2.1.1.8.html` and `https://www.codeproject.com/Articles/1058126/Memory-allocation-in-Net-Value-type-Reference-type`.

So, when you create a variable of `struct` type, that variable directly stores data instead of reference, as is the case with classes. In C#, the `struct` keyword (refer to section C# keywords for more detail) helps declare structures. Structures are helpful in representing a record or when you need to present some data.

Take a look at the following example:

```
public struct BookAuthor
{
public string Name;
public string BookTitle;
public int Age;
public string City;
public string State;
public string Country;

    //Code omitted
}
```

Here, we have a structure named `BookAuthor` that represents the data of a book author. Take a look at the following code that is consuming this structure:

```
private static void StructureExample()
{
WriteLine("Structure example\n");
Write("Author name:");
var name = ReadLine();
Write("Book Title:");
var bookTitle = ReadLine();
Write("Author age:");
var age = ReadLine();
```

```
Write("Author city:");
var city = ReadLine();
Write("Author state:");
var state = ReadLine();
Write("Author country:");
var country = ReadLine();

BookAuthor author = new
BookAuthor(name,bookTitle,Convert.ToInt32(age),city,state,country);
WriteLine($"{author.ToString()}");
BookAuthor author1 = author; //copy structure, it will copy only data as
this is //not a class

Write("Change author name:");
var name1 = ReadLine();
author.Name = name1;

WriteLine("Author1");
WriteLine($"{author.ToString()}");
WriteLine("Author2");
WriteLine($"{author1.ToString()}");
}
```

This simply displays the author details. The important point here is that once we've copied the structure, changing any field of the structure would not impact the copied contents; this is because when we copy, only the data is copied. If you perform the same operation on a class, that results in copying references instead of copying data. This copying process is called deep copy and shallow copy. Refer to `https://www.codeproject.com/Articles/28952/Shallow-Copy-vs-Deep-Copy-in-NET` in order to know more about shallow copy versus deep copy.

This is the result of the preceding code:

```
Day02 - Learn C# in 7-days
Structure example

Author name:Gaurav
Book Title:Learn C# in 7-days
Author age:43
Author city:Delhi
Author state:Delhi
Author country:India
Author Gaurav is of 43 yrs old from Delhi,Delhi,India has written book: 'Learn C# in 7-days'
Change author name:Aroraa
Author1
Author Aroraa is of 43 yrs old from Delhi,Delhi,India has written book: 'Learn C# in 7-days'
Author2
Author Gaurav is of 43 yrs old from Delhi,Delhi,India has written book: 'Learn C# in 7-days'
```

Now, let's try the same operations with the class; take a look at the following code, which consumes our class:

```
private static void StructureExample()
{
WriteLine("Structure example\n");
Write("Author name:");
var name = ReadLine();
Write("Book Title:");
var bookTitle = ReadLine();
Write("Author age:");
var age = ReadLine();
Write("Author city:");
var city = ReadLine();
Write("Author state:");
var state = ReadLine();
Write("Author country:");
var country = ReadLine();

ClassBookAuthor author = new
ClassBookAuthor(name,bookTitle,Convert.ToInt32(age),city,state,country);
WriteLine($"{author.ToString()}");
ClassBookAuthor author1 = author; //copy class, it will copy reference

Write("Change author name:");
var name1 = ReadLine();
author.Name = name1;

WriteLine("Author1");
WriteLine($"{author.ToString()}");
WriteLine("Author2");
WriteLine($"{author1.ToString()}");
}
```

Now both our class variables will have the same values. The following screenshot shows us the results:

```
Day02 - Learn C# in 7-days
Structure example

Author name:Gaurav
Book Title:Learn C# in 7-days
Author age:43
Author city:Delhi
Author state:Delhi
Author country:India
Author Gaurav is of 43 yrs old from Delhi,Delhi,India has written book: 'Learn C# in 7-days'
Change author name:Aroraa
Author1
Author Aroraa is of 43 yrs old from Delhi,Delhi,India has written book: 'Learn C# in 7-days'
Author2
Author Aroraa is of 43 yrs old from Delhi,Delhi,India has written book: 'Learn C# in 7-days'
```

Structures and classes are different:

- Structures are value types, whereas classes are reference types.
- Classes support single inheritance (multiple inheritance can be achieved using interfaces), but structures do not support inheritance.
- Classes have an implicit default constructor, but a structure does not have a default constructor.

There are more functionalities of structures that we did not discuss here. Refer to `https://docs.microsoft.com/en-us/dotnet/csharp/tour-of-csharp/structs` to get more inside information about struct.

Hands-on exercise

Let's rewind our learning for today - that is, day two - by solving the following problems:

1. Write a short program to demonstrate that we can use same class name within different namespaces.
2. Define the `console` class. Write a `console` program to display all available colors by modifying the code example discussed in the book so that all vowels will be displayed as green and all consonants as blue.
3. Elaborate on C# reserved keywords.
4. Describe different categories of C# keywords with examples.

5. Create a small program to demonstrate the `is` and `as` operators.

6. Write a short program to showcase a query expression with the help of contextual keywords.

7. Write a short program to showcase the importance of the `this` and `base` keywords.

8. Define boxing and unboxing with the help of a short program.

9. Write a short program to prove that pointer type variable stores the memory of another variable rather than data.

10. Write a short program to showcase the operator precedence order.

11. What is operator overloading? Write a short program to showcase operator overloading in action.

12. What are the operators that cannot be overloaded and why?

13. Define type conversion with the help of a short program.

14. Write a short program that uses all the available built-in C# types and perform casting using the conversion method (decimal to int conversion can be achieved using `var result = Convert.ToInt32(5689.25);`).

15. Define C# statements.

16. Write a program to elaborate each statement category.

17. What are `jump` statements? Write a small program to showcase all `jump` statements.

18. What is an array in C#?

19. Write a program and prove that an array is a block of contiguous memory.

20. Refer to `System.Array` class (https://docs.microsoft.com/en-us/dotnet/api/system.array?view=netcore-2.0) and write a short program.

21. Pass an array as a parameter to a method.

22. Sort the array.

23. Copy the array.

24. Refer to the `System.String` class and explore all its methods and properties with the help of a short program.

25. How are string objects immutable? Write a short program to showcase this.

26. What are string builders?

27. What is a class?

28. What is a structure?

29. Write a small program and showcase the differences between a `struct` and a `class`.

30. Explain compile-time type and runtime type.
31. Write a program to show the difference between compile-time type and runtime type.
32. Write a short program to prove that, explicitly, type conversion leads to data loss.

Revisiting day 2

So, we are concluding day two of our seven-day learning series. Today, we started with a very simple C# program and went through all of its parts (a typical C# program). Then, we discussed everything about C# reserved keywords and accessors and we also understand what contextual keywords are.

We covered the type casting and type conversion of various available data types in C#. You learned how boxing and unboxing happened and how we can perform conversion using inbuilt methods.

We also went through and understood various statements, and you learned the usage and flow of various statements, such as `for`, `foreach`, `while`, `do`. We looked at conditional statements, `that is`, `if`, `if...else`, `if...elseif...else` switch with the help of code examples.

We then went through arrays and understood them with the help of code examples, including string manipulations.

Finally, we concluded our day by covering structure and classes. We looked at how these two are different.

Tomorrow, on day three, we will discuss all the new features of the C# language and discuss their usage and functionality with the help of code examples.

3
Day 03 - What's New in C#

Today, we will learn a very recent and newly released feature with the current version of the C# language, that is, C# 7.0 (this is the most recent adaptation amid the review of this book). Some of these elements are altogether new and others were present in past adaptations and have been upgraded in the current version of the language. C# 7.0 will change the game with a lot of new features to the table. Some of these elements, such as tuples, are augmentations of officially accessible ideas while others are completely new. Here are the fundamental elements we will learn about on Day 03:

- Tuples and deconstruction
- Pattern matching
- Local functions
- Literal improvements
- Async Main
- Default Expressions
- Infer Tuple Names

Tuples and deconstruction

Tuples have not been newly introduced in the current version but were introduced with the .NET 4.0 release. In the present release, they have been improved.

Tuples

Tuples are there at whatever point a particular case needs to return multiple values from a method. For instance, let's say we have to find odd and even numbers from a given number series.

Tuples are an unchanging information esteem that hold related data. Tuples used to aggregate together related data, for example, such that a person's name, age, gender and whatever you want data as an information.

To complete this, our method should return or provide us the result with a number and saying whether this is an odd number or even number. For a method that will return these multiple values, we could use custom datatypes, dynamic return types, or out parameters, which sometimes will create confusion for a developer.

To use tuples, you need to add the NuGet package:

```
https://www.nuget.org/packages/System.ValueTuple/
```

For this problem, we have a tuple object and in C# 7.0 we have two different things, tuple types and tuple literals, to return multiple values from a method.

Let us discuss tuples in detail using a code example. Consider the following code snippet:

```
public static (int, string) FindOddEvenBySingleNumber(int number)
{
    string oddOrEven = IsOddNumber(number) ? "Odd" :"Even";
    return (number, oddOrEven);//tuple literal
}
```

In the preceding code snippet, the method `FindOddEvenBySingleNumber` is returning multiple values, which tells us whether a number is odd or even. See the return statement `return (number, oddOrEven)` of the preceding code: here, we are simply returning two different variables. Now, how are these values accessible from the caller method? In this case, we are returning a tuple value and the caller method will receive a tuple with these values, which are nothing but elements or items of a tuple. In this case, the number will be available as `Item1` and `oddOrEven` as `Item2` for the caller method. The following is from the caller method:

```
var result = OddEven.FindOddEvenBySingleNumber(Convert.ToInt32(number);
Console.WriteLine($"Number:{result.Item1} is {result.Item2}");
```

In the preceding code snippet, `result.Item1` represents number and `result.Item2` represents `oddOrEven`. This is fine when someone knows the representation of these tuple items/elements. But think of a scenario where we have numerous tuple elements and the developer who is writing the caller method is not aware of the representation of these items/elements. In that case, it is bit complex to consume these tuple items/elements. To overcome this problem, we can give a name to these tuple items. We call these named tuple items/elements. Let us modify our method `FindOddEvenBySingleNumber` to return named tuple items:

```
public static (int number, string oddOrEvent) FindOddEvenBySingleNumber
(int number)
{
    string result = IsOddNumber(number) ? "Odd" : "Even";
    return (number:number, oddOrEvent: result);//returning
    named tuple element in tuple literal
}
```

In the preceding code snippet, we added more descriptive names to our tuple. Now the caller method can directly use these names, as shown in the following code snippet:

```
var result = OddEven.FindOddEvenBySingle(Convert.ToInt32(number));
Console.WriteLine($"Number:{result.number} is {result.oddOrEvent}");
```

By adding some descriptive names to the tuple, we can easily identify and use items/elements of the tuple in the caller method.

The System.ValueTuple struct

Tuples in C# 7.0 require the NuGet package `System.ValueType`. This is nothing but a struct by design. This contains a few static and public methods to work undeneath:

- **CompareTo(ValueTuple)**: A public method that compares to the `ValueTuple` instance. The method returns 0 if the comparison is successful, else it returns 1.
- Here we have two methods that show the power of the `CompareTo` method:

```
public static bool CompareToTuple(int number)
{
    var oddEvenValueTuple =
    FindOddEvenBySingleNumber(number);
    var differentTupleValue =
    FindOddEvenBySingleNumberNamedElement(number + 1);
    var res =
    oddEvenValueTuple.CompareTo(differentTupleValue);
    return res == 0; // 0 if other is a ValueTuple instance
```

```
       and 1 if other is null
    }
    public static bool CompareToTuple1(int number)
    {
        var oddEvenValueTuple =
        FindOddEvenBySingleNumber(number);
        var sameTupleValue =
        FindOddEvenBySingleNumberNamedElement(number);
        var res = oddEvenValueTuple.CompareTo(sameTupleValue);
        return res == 0;// 0 if other is a ValueTuple instance
        and 1 if other is null
    }
```

Here is the calling code snippet to get the results from preceding code:

```
Console.Clear();
Console.Write("Enter number: ");
var num = Console.ReadLine();
var resultNum =
OddEven.FindOddEvenBySingleNumberNamedElement(Convert.ToInt32(n
um));
Console.WriteLine($"Number:{resultNum.number} is
{resultNum.oddOrEven}.");
Console.WriteLine();
var comp = OddEven.CompareToTuple(Convert.ToInt32(num));
Console.WriteLine($"Comparison of two Tuple objects having
different value is:{comp}");
var comp1 = OddEven.CompareToTuple1(Convert.ToInt32(num));
Console.WriteLine($"Comparison of two Tuple objects having same
value is:{comp1}");
```

When we execute the preceding code, it will provide the output as follows:

```
Enter number: 5
Number:5 is Odd.

Comparison of two Tuple objects having different value is:False
Comparison of two Tuple objects having same value is:True
Press any key...
```

- **Equals(Object):** A public method that returns true/false, stating whether the TupleValue instance is equal to the provided object. It returns true if successful.

- The following is the implementation:

```
public static bool EqualToTuple(int number)
{
    var oddEvenValueTuple =
    FindOddEvenBySingleNumber(number);
    var sameTupleValue =
    FindOddEvenBySingleNumberNamedElement(number);
    var res = oddEvenValueTuple.Equals(sameTupleValue);
    return res;//true if obj is a ValueTuple instance;
    otherwise, false.
}
```

Here is the calling method code snippet:

```
var num1 = Console.ReadLine();
var namedElement =
OddEven.FindOddEvenBySingleNumberNamedElement(Convert.ToInt32(n
um1));
Console.WriteLine($"Number:{namedElement.number} is
{namedElement.oddOrEven}.");
Console.WriteLine();
var equalToTuple = OddEven.EqualToTuple(Convert.ToInt32(num1));
Console.WriteLine($"Equality of two Tuple objects
is:{equalToTuple}");
var equalToObject =
OddEven.EqualToObject(Convert.ToInt32(num1));
Console.WriteLine($"Equality of one Tuple object with other non
tuple object is:{equalToObject}");
```

Finally, the output is as follows:

```
Enter number: 5
Number:5 is Odd.

Comparison of two Tuple objects having different value is:False
Comparison of two Tuple objects having same value is:True
Press any key...
```

- **Equals(ValueTuple)**: A public method that always returns true and it's by design. It is designed in this way because `ValueTuple` is a zero-element tuple, hence when two ValueTuples perform equally having no element will always return zero.

- **GetHashCode()**: A public method that returns the hash code of the object.
- **GetType()**: A public method that provides the specific type of the current instance.
- **ToString()**: A public method that is a string representation of the `ValueTuple` instance. However, as per design, it always returns zero.
- **Create()**: A static method that creates a new `ValueTuple` (0 tuple). We can create a 0 tuple as follows:

```
public static ValueTuple CreateValueTuple() =>
ValueTuple.Create();
```

- **Create<T1>(T1) ...**
  Create<T1, T2, T3, T4, T5, T6, T7, T8>(T1, T2, T3, T4, T5, T6, T7, T8): All are static methods which create Value Tuples with 1-components (singleton) to 8-components (octuple).
- See the following code snippet showing singleton and octuple examples:

```
public static ValueTuple<int> CreateValueTupleSingleton(int
number) => ValueTuple.Create(number);
public static ValueTuple<int, int, int, int, int, int, int,
ValueTuple<int,string>> OctupleUsingCreate() =>
ValueTuple.Create(1, 2, 3, 4, 5, 6, 7, ValueTuple.Create(8,
IsOddNumber(8) ? "Odd" : "Even"));
```

 You will need to update the NuGet package to Microsoft.Net.Compilers to 2.0 preview if you get compilation warnings. To do so, just select **preview** and search Microsoft.Net.Compilers to 2.0 from NuGet Package Manager [https://www.nuget.org/packages/Microsoft.Net.Compilers/].

Deconstruction

In the preceding section, we saw that multiple return values with the use of `ValueTuple` are accessible with its items/element. Now think of a scenario where we want to directly assign these element values to variables. Here, deconstruction helps us. Deconstruction is a way in which we can unpackage the tuple that is returned by a method.

There are mainly two ways to deconstruct a tuple:

- Explicitly typed declaration: We explicitly declare the type of each field. Let's see the following code example:

```
public static string ExplicitlyTypedDeconstruction(int num)
{
    (int number, string evenOdd) =
    FindOddEvenBySingleNumber(num);
    return $"Entered number:{number} is {evenOdd}.";
}
```

- Implicitly typed declaration: We implicitly declare the type of each field. Let's see the following code example:

```
public static string ImplicitlyTypedDeconstruction(int num)
{
    var (number, evenOdd) =
    FindOddEvenBySingleNumber(num);
    //Following deconstruct is also valid
    //(int number, var evenOdd) =
    FindOddEvenBySingleNumber(num);
    return $"Entered number:{number} is {evenOdd}.";
}
```

We can also deconstruct UserDefined/Custom types by implementing deconstruction using out parameters; see the following code-example:

```
public static string UserDefinedTypeDeconstruction(int num)
{
    var customModel = new UserDefinedModel(num,
    IsOddNumber(num) ? "Odd" : "Even");
    var (number, oddEven) = customModel;
    return $"Entered number:{number} is {oddEven}.";
}
```

In the preceding code, the deconstruct method enables assignment from a `UserDefinedModel` to one int and one string, which represent the properties `number` and `OddEven` respectively.

Tuple – important points to remember

In the preceding section, we discussed tuples and noticed how they help us in scenarios where we need multiple values and complex data values (besides custom types). Here are the important points that we should remember while working with tuples:

- To work with tuples, we need the NuGet package `System.ValueTuple`.
- `ValueTuple` (`System.ValueTuple`) is a struct instead of a class by design.
- `ValueTuple` implements `IEquatable<ValueTuple>`, `IStructuralEquatable`, `IStructuralComparable`, `IComparable`, `IComparable<ValueTuple>` interfaces.
- ValueTuples are mutable.
- ValueTuples are flexible data containers and can be either unnamed or named:

  - **Unnamed**: When we do not provide any name for a field, these are unnamed tuples and accessible using the default fields `Item1`, `Item2`, and so on:

    ```
    var oddNumber = (3, "Odd"); //Unnamed tuple
    ```

  - **Named**: When we explicitly provide some descriptive name to fields:

    ```
    var oddNumber = (number: 3, oddOrEven: "Odd"); //Named
    Tuple
    ```

- Assignment: When we assign one tuple to another, only values get assigned and not field names:

  ```
  Console.Write("Enter first number: ");
  var userInputFirst = Console.ReadLine();
  Console.Write("Enter second number: ");
  var userInputSecond = Console.ReadLine();
  var noNamed =
  OddEven.FindOddEvenBySingleNumber(Convert.ToInt32(userInputFirs
  t));
  var named =
  OddEven.FindOddEvenBySingleNumberNamedElement(Convert.ToInt32(u
  serInputSecond));
  Console.WriteLine($"First Number:{noNamed.Item1} is
  {noNamed.Item2} using noNamed tuple.");
  Console.WriteLine($"Second Number:{named.number} is
  {named.oddOrEven} using Named tuple.");
  ```

```
Console.WriteLine("Assigning 'Named' to 'NoNamed'");
                          noNamed = named;
Console.WriteLine($"Number:{noNamed.Item1} is {named.Item2}
after assignment.");
Console.Write("Enter third number: ");
var userInputThird = Console.ReadLine();
var noNamed2 =
OddEven.FindOddEvenBySingleNumber(Convert.ToInt32(userInputThir
d));
Console.WriteLine($"Third Number:{noNamed2.Item1} is
{noNamed2.Item2} using second noNamed tuple.");
Console.WriteLine("Assigning 'second NoNamed' to 'Named'");
named = noNamed2;
Console.WriteLine($"Second Number:{named.number} is
{named.oddOrEven} after assignment.");
```

The output of the preceding code-snippet would be as follows:

```
Enter first number: 3
Enter second number: 5
First Number:3 is Odd using noNamed tuple.
Second Number:5 is Odd using Named tuple.
Assigning 'Named' to 'NoNamed'
Number:5 is Odd after assignment.
Enter third number: 6
Third Number:6 is Even using second noNamed tuple.
Assigning 'second NoNamed' to 'Named'
Second Number:6 is Even after assignment.
Press any key...
```

In the preceding code-snippet, we can see that the output of an assigned tuple is the same with an assigned tuple.

Pattern matching

In a general way, pattern matching is a way to compare contents in predefined formats in an expression. The format is nothing but a combination of different matches.

In C# 7.0, pattern matching is a feature. With the use of this feature, we can implement method dispatch on properties other than the type of an object.

Pattern matching supports various expressions; let's discuss these with code-examples.

 Patterns can be constant patterns: Type patterns or Var patterns.

is expression

The `is` expression enables the inspection of an object and its properties and determines whether it satisfies the pattern:

```
public static string MatchingPatterUsingIs(object character)
{
    if (character is null)
    return $"{nameof(character)} is null. ";
    if (character is char)
    {
        var isVowel = IsVowel((char) character) ? "is a
        vowel" : "is a consonent";
        return $"{character} is char and {isVowel}. ";
    }
    if (character is string)
    {
        var chars = ((string) character).ToArray();
        var stringBuilder = new StringBuilder();
        foreach (var c in chars)
        {
            if (!char.IsWhiteSpace(c))
            {
            var isVowel = IsVowel(c) ? "is a vowel" : "is a
            consonent";
            stringBuilder.AppendLine($"{c} is char of string
            '{character}' and {isVowel}.");
            }
        }

        return stringBuilder.ToString();
    }
    throw new ArgumentException(
    "character is not a recognized data type.",
    nameof(character));
}
```

The preceding code is not showing any fancy stuff and informs us whether the input parameter is a specific type and a vowel or a consonant. You can see here we simply use the `is` operator, that tells whether the object is of the same type or not.

 The `is` operator (`https://goo.gl/79sLW5`) checks the object, and if the object is of the same type, it returns true; if not, it returns false.

In the preceding code, while we are checking object for string, we need to explicitly cast object to string and then pass this to our utility method, `IsVowel()`. In the preceding code, we are doing two things: the first is checking the type of the incoming parameter and if the type is the same then we are casting it to the desired type and performing actions as per our case. Sometimes this creates confusion when we need to write more complex logic with expressions.

C# 7.0 resolves this subtly to make our expression simpler. Now we can directly declare a variable while checking the type in an expression; see the following code:

```
if (character is string str)
{
    var chars = str.ToArray();
    var stringBuilder = new StringBuilder();
    foreach (var c in chars)
    {
        if (!char.IsWhiteSpace(c))
        {
            var isVowel = IsVowel(c) ? "is a vowel" : "is
            a consonent";
            stringBuilder.AppendLine($"{c} is char of
            string '{character}' and {isVowel}.");
        }
    }

    return stringBuilder.ToString();
}
```

In the preceding code, which is updated where the `is` expression both tests the variable and assigns it to a new variable of the desired type. With this change, there is no need to explicitly cast the type (`(string) character`) as we were doing in the previous code.

Let us add one more condition to the preceding code:

```
if (character is int number)
return $"{nameof(character)} is int {number}.";
```

In the preceding code, we are checking *object* for int, which is a *struct*. The preceding condition works perfectly fine and produces the expected results.

Here is our complete code:

```
private static IEnumerable<char> Vowels => new[] {'a', 'e', 'i', 'o', 'u'};

public static string MatchingPatterUsingIs(object character)
{
    if (character is null)
    return $"{nameof(character)} is null. ";
    if (character is char)
    {
        var isVowel = IsVowel((char) character) ? "is a
        vowel" : "is a consonent";
        return $"{character} is char and {isVowel}. ";
    }
    if (character is string str)
    {
        var chars = str.ToArray();
        var stringBuilder = new StringBuilder();
        foreach (var c in chars)
        {
            if (!char.IsWhiteSpace(c))
            {
                var isVowel = IsVowel(c) ? "is a vowel" :
                "is a consonent";
                stringBuilder.AppendLine($"{c} is char of
                string '{character}' and {isVo
            }
        }

        return stringBuilder.ToString();
    }

    if (character is int number)
    return $"{nameof(character)} is int {number}.";

    throw new ArgumentException(
    "character is not a recognized data type.",
    nameof(character));
}

private static bool IsVowel(char character) =>
Vowels.Contains(char.ToLower(character));
```

The is expression works perfectly fine with both value types as well as reference types.

In the preceding code-example, the variables str and number are only assigned when the respective expression matches results as true.

switch statement

We have already discussed the switch statement in Day 02. The switch pattern helps a great deal as it uses any datatype for matching additionally case provides a way so, it matched the condition.

The match expression is the same but in C# 7.0, this feature has been enhanced in three different ways. Let us understand them using code examples.

constant pattern

In earlier versions of C#, the switch statement only supported the *constant* pattern, where we evaluate some variable in the switch and then make a conditional call as per the constant case. See the following code example, where we are trying to check whether inputChar is of a specific length, which is computed in switch:

```
public static string ConstantPatternUsingSwitch(params char[] inputChar)
{
    switch (inputChar.Length)
    {

        case 0:
            return $"{nameof(inputChar)} contains no
            elements.";
        case 1:
            return $"'{inputChar[0]}' and
            {VowelOrConsonent(inputChar[0])}.";
        case 2:
            var sb = new
            StringBuilder().AppendLine($"'{inputChar[0]}'
            and {VowelOrConsonent(inputChar[0])}.");
            sb.AppendLine($"'{inputChar[1]}' and
            {VowelOrConsonent(inputChar[1])}.");
            return sb.ToString();
        case 3:
```

```
              var sb1 = new
              StringBuilder().AppendLine($"'{inputChar[0]}'
              and {VowelOrConsonent(inputChar[0])}.");
              sb1.AppendLine($"'{inputChar[1]}' and
              {VowelOrConsonent(inputChar[1])}.");
              sb1.AppendLine($"'{inputChar[2]}' and
              {VowelOrConsonent(inputChar[2])}.");
              return sb1.ToString();
          case 4:
              var sb2 = new
              StringBuilder().AppendLine($"'{inputChar[0]}'
              and {VowelOrConsonent(inputChar[0])}.");
              sb2.AppendLine($"'{inputChar[1]}' and
              {VowelOrConsonent(inputChar[1])}.");
              sb2.AppendLine($"'{inputChar[2]}' and
              {VowelOrConsonent(inputChar[2])}.");
              sb2.AppendLine($"'{inputChar[3]}' and
              {VowelOrConsonent(inputChar[3])}.");
              return sb2.ToString();
          case 5:
              var sb3 = new
              StringBuilder().AppendLine($"'{inputChar[0]}'
              and {VowelOrConsonent(inputChar[0])}.");
              sb3.AppendLine($"'{inputChar[1]}' and
              {VowelOrConsonent(inputChar[1])}.");
              sb3.AppendLine($"'{inputChar[2]}' and
              {VowelOrConsonent(inputChar[2])}.");
              sb3.AppendLine($"'{inputChar[3]}' and
              {VowelOrConsonent(inputChar[3])}.");
              sb3.AppendLine($"'{inputChar[4]}' and
              {VowelOrConsonent(inputChar[4])}.");
              return sb3.ToString();
          default:
              return $"{inputChar.Length} exceeds from
              maximum input length.";
      }
  }
```

In the preceding code, our main task is to check whether `inputChar` is a vowel or consonant, and what we are doing here is we are first evaluating the length of the `inputChar` and then performing operations as required, which leads to more work/code for more complex conditions.

type pattern

With the introduction of the *type* pattern, we can overcome the problem we were facing with the *constant* pattern (in the previous section). Consider the following code:

```
public static string TypePatternUsingSwitch(IEnumerable<object>
inputObjects)
{
    var message = new StringBuilder();
    foreach (var inputObject in inputObjects)
    switch (inputObject)
        {
            case char c:
                message.AppendLine($"{c} is char and
                {VowelOrConsonent(c)}.");
                break;
            case IEnumerable<object> listObjects:
                foreach (var listObject in listObjects)
                message.AppendLine(MatchingPatterUsingIs(
                listObject));
                break;
            case null:
                break;
        }
    return message.ToString();
}
```

In the preceding code, now it's easy to perform the operation as per type pattern.

When clause in case expression

With the introduction of a `when` clause in `case` expressions, you can do special things in the expression; see the following code:

```
public static string TypePatternWhenInCaseUsingSwitch(IEnumerable<object>
inputObjects)
{
    var message = new StringBuilder();
    foreach (var inputObject in inputObjects)
    switch (inputObject)
        {
            case char c:
                message.AppendLine($"{c} is char and
                {VowelOrConsonent(c)}.");
                break;
            case IEnumerable<object> listObjects when
```

```
                        listObjects.Any():
                        foreach (var listObject in listObjects)
                        message.AppendLine(MatchingPatterUsingIs
                        (listObject));
                        break;
                case IEnumerable<object> listInlist:
                        break;
                case null:
                        break;
            }
        return message.ToString();
    }
```

In the preceding code, `case` with `when` makes sure that it will perform the operation only if `listObjects` has some value.

 The `case` statement requires that each `case` ends with a `break`, `return`, or `goto`.

Local functions

Local functions can be achievable using function and action using anonymous methods in prior versions, but there are still a few limitations:

- Generics
- `ref` and `out` parameters
- `params`

Local functions are featured to declare within the block scope. These functions are very powerful and have the same capability as any other normal function but with the difference that they are scoped within the block these were declared.

Consider the following code-example:

```
public static string FindOddEvenBySingleNumber(int number) =>
IsOddNumber(number) ? "Odd" : "Even";
```

The method `FindOddEvenBySingleNumber()` in the preceding code is simply returning a number as *Odd* or *Even* for numbers greater than 1. This uses a private method, `IsOddNumber()`, as shown here:

```
private static bool IsOddNumber(int number) => number >= 1 && number % 2 !=
0;
```

The method `IsOddNumber()` is a private method and is available within the class it declared. Hence, its scope is within a class and not within a code block.

Let us see the following code-example of a local function:

```
public string FindOddEvenBySingleNumberUsingLocalFunction(int someInput)
{
    //Local function, scoped within
    FindOddEvenBySingleNumberUsingLocalFunction
    bool IsOddNumber(int number)
    {
        return number >= 1 && number % 2 != 0;
    }

    return IsOddNumber(someInput) ? "Odd" : "Even";
}
```

In the preceding code, the local function `IsOddNumber()` is performing the same action as in the case of the `private` method in the previous section. But here, the scope of `IsOddNumber()` is within the method `FindOddEvenBySingleNumberUsingLocalFunction()`. Hence, it would not be available outside this code block.

Literal improvements

When it comes to literals, we can think about the declaration of various variables constant, which are sometimes the life of a method as these would be very important for a method or to take any decision. And it leads to wrong decisions with the misreading of a numeric constant. To overcome this confusion, C# 7.0 introduced two new features, binary literals and digit separators.

Binary literals

Binary digits are very important for performing complex operations. A constant of a binary digit can be declared as *0b<binaryvalue>*, where 0b tells us that this is a binary literal and binary values is the value of your decimal digit. Here are a few examples:

```
//Binary literals
public const int Nineteen = 0b00010011;
public const int Ten = 0b00001010;
public const int Four = 0b0100;
public const int Eight = 0b1000;
```

Digit separator

With the introduction of digit separators, we can easily read long numeric, binary digits. Digit separators can be used with both numeric and binary digits. For binary digits, the digit separator, that is, underscore (_), applies on bit pattern, and for numeric, it can appear anywhere but it is good to make 1,000 the separator. Take a look at the following examples:

```
//Digit separator - Binary numbers
public const int Hundred = 0b0110_0100;
public const int Fifty = 0b0011_0010;
public const int Twenty = 0b0001_0100;
//Numeric separator
public const long Billion = 100_000_0000;
```

 The digit separator can be used with decimal, float, and double types as well.

<p>Followings are the new features shipped with Visual Studio 2017 update 3 as a language features of C# 7.1, we will discuss all the features as per: https://github.com/dotnet/roslyn/blob/master/docs/Language%20Feature%20Status.md

 For more information new release of Visual Stuio 2017 refer to: https://www.visualstudio.com/en-us/news/releasenotes/vs2017-relnotes

If you are looking how to set up your existing project or new project that is using C# 7.0 – then you need not to worry, Visual Studio 2017 Update 3 is there to assist you. Whenever you start using new feature of C# 7.1 – you need to follow these steps:

1. Visual Studio will warn about existing version support and suggest to upgrade your project if you want to use new feature of C# 7.1.
2. Just click on yellow bulb and select best option fits for your requirement and you're good to go with new C# 7.1.

Following image tells you two-steps to get ready with C# 7.1:

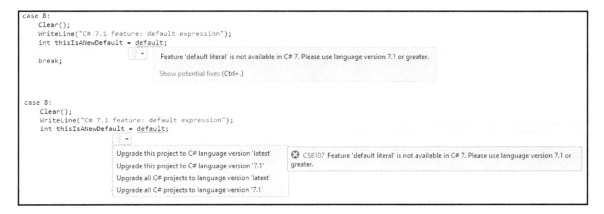

Let us start discussion on new features of Language C# 7.1:

Async Main

A new feature of language C# 7.1 that enables entry-point that is, Main of an application. Async main enables main method to be awaitable that mean Main method is now asynchronous to get Task or Task<int>. With this feature followings are valid entry-points:

```
static Task Main()
{
    //stuff goes here
}
static Task<int> Main()
{
    //stuff goes here
}
static Task Main(string[] args)
{
    //stuff goes here
}
static Task<int> Main(string[] args)
```

```
{
    //stuff goes here
}
```

Restrictions while using new signatures

- You can use these new signature entry-points and these marked as valid if no overload of previous signature is present that means if you are using an existing entry-point.

```
public static void Main()
{
    NewMain().GetAwaiter().GetResult();
}
private static async Task NewMain()
{
    //async stuff goes here
}
```

- This is not mandatory to mark your entry-point as async that means you can still use the existing async entry-point:

```
private static void Main(string[] args)
{
    //stuff goes here
}
```

 There may be more usage of the entry-point that you can incorporate in the application – refer to official document of this feature: https://github.com/dotnet/csharplang/blob/master/proposals/async-main.md

Default expressions

A new expression introduced in C# 7.1 that is default literal. With the introduction of this new literal, the expression can be implicitly converted to any type and produces result as default value of the type.

 New default literal is different than old default(T). Earlier default convert the target type of T but newer one can convert any type.

Following is the code-snippet that is showing both old and new `default`:

```
//Code removed
case 8:
    Clear();
    WriteLine("C# 7.1 feature: default expression");
    int thisIsANewDefault = default;
    var thisIsAnOlderDefault = default(int);
    WriteLine($"New default:{thisIsANewDefault}. Old
    default:{thisIsAnOlderDefault}");
    PressAnyKey();
    break;
//Code removed
```

In the preceding code when we are writing `int thisIsANewDefault = default;` an expression that is valid in C# 7.1 and it implicitly convert the expression to type int and assign a default value that is 0 (zero) to `thisIsANewDefault`. The notable point here is that default literal implicitly detect the type of `thisIsANewDefault` and set the value. On the other hand, we need to explicitly tell the target type to set the default value in expression `var thisIsAnOlderDefault = default(int);`.

The preceding code generates following output:

```
Example - Day03

1. Odd Even from a Single Number
2. Odd Even within a Range
3. Odd Even from a Series
4. Assignment
5. Implicit Cast
6. Comparison
7. Equals
8. Default Expression (C# 7.1)
9. Exit
Enter choice (1-9): 8

C# 7.1 feature: default expression
New default:0. Old default:0
Press any key...
```

There are multiple implementations of new default literal so, you can use the same with following:

Member variables

New `default` expression can be applied to assign default values to variables, followings are the various ways:

```
int thisIsANewDefault = default;
int thisIsAnOlderDefault = default(int);
var thisIsAnOlderDefaultAndStillValid = default(int);
var thisIsNotValid = default; //Not valid, as we cannot assign default to
implicit-typed variable
```

Constants

Similar to variables, with the use of default we can declare constants, followings are the various ways:

```
const int thisIsANewDefaultConst = default; //valid
const int thisIsAnOlderDefaultCont = default(int); //valid
const int? thisIsInvalid = default; //Invalid, as nullable cannot be
declared const
```

 There are more scenarios where you can use this new default literal viz. optional parameter in method that is, For more information, refer to: https://github.com/dotnet/csharplang/blob/master/meetings/2017/ LDM-2017-03-07.md

Infer tuple names

With the introduction of this new feature we you do not require to explicitly declare the tuple candidate names. We discussed Tuples in previous section *Tuples and Deconstructions*. Infer tuple names feature is an extended to the tuple values introduced in C# 7.0.

To work with this new feature, you require updated NuGet package of `ValueTuple` that you've installed in previous section *Tuple*. To update the NuGet package, go to *NuGet Package manager* and click on **Update** tab and then click **update latest version**. Following screenshot provides the complete information:

Following code-snippet shows, various ways to declare the tuple:

```
public static void InferTupleNames(int num1, int num2)
{
    (int, int) noNamed = (num1, num2);
    (int, int) IgnoredName = (A:num1, B:num2);
    (int a, int b) typeNamed = (num1, num2);
    var named = (num1, num2);
    var noNamedVariation = (num1, num1);
    var explicitNaming = (n: num1, num1);
    var partialnamed = (num1, 5);
}
```

The preceding code is self-explanatory, Tuple `noNamed` does not have any member name and can be accessed using `item1` and `item2`. Similarly, in Tuple `IgnoredName` all defined member names will be ignored as declaration is not defined with a member name. Following code-snippet tells the complete story of how we can access various tuples:

```
public static void InferTupleNames(int num1, int num2)
{
    (int, int) noNamed = (num1, num2);
    Console.WriteLine($"NoNamed:{noNamed.Item1},
    {noNamed.Item2}");
    (int, int) ignoredName = (A:num1, B:num2);
    Console.WriteLine($"IgnoredName:{ignoredName.Item1}
    ,{ignoredName.Item2}");
    (int a, int b) typeNamed = (num1, num2);
    Console.WriteLine($"typeNamed using default member-
    names:{typeNamed.Item1}
    {typeNamed.Item2}");
    Console.WriteLine($"typeNamed:{typeNamed.a},
    {typeNamed.b}");
```

```
        var named = (num1, num2);
        Console.WriteLine($"named using default member-names
        :{named.Item1},{named.Item2}");
        Console.WriteLine($"named:{named.num1},{named.num2}");
        var noNamedVariation = (num1, num1);
        Console.WriteLine($"noNamedVariation:
        {noNamedVariation.Item1},{noNamedVariation.Item2}");
        var explicitNaming = (n: num1, num1);
        Console.WriteLine($"explicitNaming:{explicitNaming.n},
        {explicitNaming.num1}");
        var partialnamed = (num1, 5);
        Console.WriteLine($"partialnamed:{partialnamed.num1},
        {partialnamed.Item2}");
    }
```

The preceding code produces the following output:

```
Example - Day03

1. Odd Even from a Single Number
2. Odd Even within a Range
3. Odd Even from a Series
4. Assignment
5. Implicit Cast
6. Comparison
7. Equals
8. Default Expression (C# 7.1)
9. Infer tuple names (C# 7.1)
10. Exit
Enter choice (1-10): 9.

C# 7.1 feature: Infer tuple names
Enter first number:58
Enter second number:98
NoNamed:58,98
IgnoredName:58,98
typeNamed using default member-names:58,98
typeNamed:58,98
named using default member-names:58,98
named:58,98
noNamedVariation:58,58
explicitNaming:58,58
partialnamed:58,5
Press any key...
```

There is more variation where you can use this new feature for more info, refer: https://github.com/dotnet/roslyn/blob/master/docs/features/tuples.md

Other features supposed to release

There would be more features with the final release of programming language C# 7.1 in addition to previous, following are the features that encountered a bug or partially implemented as on date.

Pattern-matching with generics

The pattern-matching with generic is proposed here: https://github.com/dotnet/csharplang/blob/master/proposals/generics-pattern-match.md as new feature of C# 7.1 that encountered a bug and can be seen here: https://github.com/dotnet/roslyn/issues/16195

The implementation of this feature would be based on as operator as detailed here: https://github.com/dotnet/csharplang/blob/master/spec/expressions.md#the-as-operator

Reference assemblies

Reference assemblies feature is yet to be incorporated within IDE, you can refer: https://github.com/dotnet/roslyn/blob/master/docs/features/refout.md here for more details.

Hands-on exercises

Answer the following questions, which cover the concepts of today's learning:

1. What are ValueTuple types?
2. ValueTuples are mutable; prove with an example.
3. Create a ValueTuple of 10 elements.

4. Create a user-defined class employee as follows and then write a program to deconstruct user-defined types:

```
public class employee
{
public Guid EmplId { get; set; }
public String First { get; set; }
public string Last { get; set; }
public char Sex { get; set; }
public string DepartmentId { get; set; }
public string Designation { get; set; }
}
```

5. Create a class of various constants using digit separators and implement these constants to a function `ToDecimal()` and `ToBinary()`.

6. What are local functions? How are they different from private functions?

7. Rewrite the `OddEven` program using generic local functions.

8. Rewrite the `OddEven` program using the type pattern in `switch` case.

9. Write a program to find out `OddEven` with the utilization of inferred Tuple names feature of language C# 7.1.

10. What is default expression (C# 7.1), elaborate with the help of program?

Revisiting Day 03

Today, we have discussed all the new features introduced in C# 7.0 with code examples. We also understood the important points and usage of these features.

We discussed how ValueTuples help us gather the data information and the cases where we are expecting multiple outputs from a method. One of the good points of `ValueTuple` is that this is a mutable and `ValueType`. There are a few `public` and `static` methods provided by `System.ValueTuple` and we can achieve many complex scenarios with the use of these.

Then we came to know the advantage and power of pattern matching; this helps the coder perform various complex conditional scenarios which were not possible in prior versions of the C# language. The type pattern and the `when` clause in `case` statements makes this feature superb.

Local functions are one of the most important features introduced in C# 7.0. They help a lot in a scenario, where we need to make our code symmetric, so you can read code perfectly and when we do not require the method outside, or we do not need to reuse this operation which is required within a block scope.

With the literal improvements, now we can declare binary numbers as constants and use them as we use other variables. The capability of adding the digit separator underscore (_) made this feature more useful.

Finally, we have gone through the new features released for language C# 7.1 as a part of Visual Studio update 3.

Earlier, in plan there were more features which were planned to release but the final release came with preceding new features. Next release is in plan and there are more robust features which are yet to come. You can watch the plan and next release feature list here: `https://github.com/dotnet/csharplang/tree/master/proposals`.

4

Day 04 - Discussing C# Class Members

We are in day four of our seven-day learning series. On day two, we discussed the typical C# program, and you understood how to compile and execute the program. We discussed the `Main` method and its use. We also discussed the reserved keywords of language C#, and then, we got an overview of classes and structures in C#. On day three, we discussed all the new features introduced in C#7.0.

In this chapter, the fundamentals of C# methods and properties will be explained, and we will also cover the concept of indexers in C#. The string manipulation discussed on day two will be extended through RegEx, and we will explain why it is powerful. File management will be covered along with some medium-level file system observers.

Today, we will cover C# classes in more depth. This chapter will cover the following topics:

- Modifiers
- Methods
- Properties
- Indexers
- File I/O
- Exception handling
- Discussing regular expression and its importance

On day two, we discussed a typical C# program, and we discussed how a program can be compiled and executed. What is the use/importance of the `Main` method? We will carry forward the same discussion and start our day four.

Before we start, let's go through the steps of our program in the String calculator (`https://github.com/garora/TDD-Katas/tree/develop/Src/cs/StringCalculator`). There is a simple requirement to add numbers that are provided as a string. Here is a simple code snippet on the basis of this one-liner requirement that does not mention how many numbers are needed to be supplied in a string:

```
namespace Day04
{
    class Program
    {
        static void Main(string[] args)
        {
            Write("Enter number1:");
            var num1 = ReadLine();
            Write("Enter number2:");
            var num2 = ReadLine();
            var sum = Convert.ToInt32(num1) +
            Convert.ToInt32(num2);
            Write($"Sum of {num1} and {num2} is {sum}");
            ReadLine();
        }
    }
}
```

We will get the following output when we run the preceding code:

```
Enter number1:55
Enter number2:55
Sum of 55 and 55 is 110
```

The preceding code is working fine and giving us the expected results. The requirements that we discussed previously are very limited and vague. Let's elaborate on the initial requirement:

- Create a simple String calculator with the Add operation:
    - This operation should only accept input in a string data type.
    - The Add operation can take zero, one, or two comma-separated numbers and will return their sum, for example, *1* or *1,2*.
    - The Add operation should accept an empty string, but for an empty string, it will return zero.

The preceding requirements are unanswered in our previous code snippet. To achieve these requirements, we should tweak our code snippet, which we will discuss in the upcoming sections.

Modifiers

Modifiers are nothing but special keywords in C# that are used to declare how a specific method, property, or variable could be accessible. In this section, we will discuss modifiers and discuss their usage with the use of code examples.

 The whole point of modifiers is encapsulation. It's about how objects get simplified by encapsulations, and modifiers are like knobs saying how much you want to show to some clients, and how much not to. To understand encapsulation, refer to day seven, *Encapsulation*.

Access modifiers and accessibility levels

Access modifiers tell us how and where a member, declared type, and so on can be accessed or available. The following discussion will give you a broader idea of all access modifiers and accessibility levels.

public

A `public` modifier helps us define the scope of the member without any restrictions. This means if we define any class, method, property, or variable with a public access modifier, the member can be accessed without any restrictions for other members.

 The accessibility level of the type or the member of derived type that is declared using the public access modifier is unrestricted, which means it can be accessible anywhere.

To understand unrestricted accessibility levels, let's consider following code example:

```
namespace Day04
{
    internal class StringCalculator
    {
        public string Num1 { get; set; }
        public string Num2 { get; set; }
```

```
            public int Sum() => Convert.ToInt32(Num1) + Convert.ToInt32(Num2);
    }
}
```

In the preceding code snippet, we declared two properties, `Num1` and `Num2`, and one method `Sum()`, with the access modifier `public`. This means these properties and the method is accessible to other classes as well. Here is the code snippet that consumes the preceding class:

```
namespace Day04
{
    class Program
    {
        static void Main(string[] args)
        {
            StringCalculator calculator = new
            StringCalculator();
            Write("Enter number1:");
            calculator.Num1 = ReadLine();
            Write("Enter number2:");
            calculator.Num2 = ReadLine();
            Write($"Sum of {calculator.Num1} and
            {calculator.Num2} is {calculator.Sum()}");
            ReadLine();
        }
    }
}
```

The preceding code snippet will run perfectly and produce the expected results. When you run the preceding code, it will show results, as in the following image:

```
Enter number1:208
Enter number2:109
Sum of 208 and 109 is 317
```

protected

A `protected` modifier helps us define the scope of the member without the class or type defined/created from the class where the member is defined. In other words, when we define the variable, property, or method with the access modifier `protected`, this means the scope of availability of these are within the class in which all these members are defined.

 The accessibility level of the type or the member of derived type that is declared using protected access modifiers is restricted, which means it can only be accessible within the class or from the derived types that are created from class of the member. The protected modifier is importantly and actively responsible in OOPS using C#. You should get an idea of inheritance. Refer to day seven, *Inheritance*.

To understand protected accessibility levels, let's consider the following code example:

```
namespace Day04
{
    class StringCalculator
    {

        protected string Num1 { get; set; }
        protected string Num2 { get; set; }

    }

    class StringCalculatorImplementation : StringCalculator
    {
        public void Sum()
        {
            StringCalculatorImplementation calculator =
            new StringCalculatorImplementation();

            Write("Enter number1:");

            calculator.Num1 = ReadLine();

            Write("Enter number2:");

            calculator.Num2 = ReadLine();

            int sum = Convert.ToInt32(calculator.Num1) +
            Convert.ToInt32(calculator.Num2);

            Write($"Sum of {calculator.Num1} and
            {calculator.Num2} is {sum}");
        }
```

```
        }
    }
```

In the preceding code, we have two classes: StringCalculator and StringCalculatorImplementation. Properties are defined with the protected access modifier in the StringCalculator class. This means these properties are only accessible either from the StringCalculator class or the StringCalculatorImplementation (this is a derived type of the StringCalculatorclass). The preceding code will produce the following output:

```
Enter number1:85
Enter number2:91
Sum of 85 and 91 is 176
```

The following code will not work and will produce a compile-time error:

```
class StringCalculatorImplementation : StringCalculator
{
    readonly StringCalculator _stringCalculator = new
    StringCalculator();
    public int Sum()
    {
        var num=_stringCalculator.Num1; //will not work
        var number=_stringCalculator.Num2; //will not work

        //other stuff
    }
}
```

In the preceding code, we tried to access `Num1` and `Num2` from the `StringCalculatorImplementation` class by creating an instance of the `StringCalculator` class. This is not possible and will not work. Refer to the following screenshot:

```
class StringCalculatorImplementation : StringCalculator
{
    readonly StringCalculator _stringCalculator = new StringCalculator();
    public int Sum()
    {
        var num = _stringCalculator.Num1; //will not work
        var num2 = _stringCalcul        Cannot access protected member 'StringCalculator.Num1' via a qualifier of type 'StringCalculator'; the qualifier must be of type 'StringCalculatorImplementation' (or derived from it)
        StringCalculatorImplementa    Cannot access protected property 'Num1' here
        return Convert.ToInt32(imp
    }
}
```

internal

An internal modifier helps us define the scope of the member for the same assembly. Members that are defined using internal access modifiers cannot access outside of the assembly where they are defined.

 The accessibility level of the type or the member that is declared using internal access modifiers is restricted for outside the assembly. This means these members are not allowed to access from external assemblies.

To understand internal accessibility levels, let's consider the following code example:

```
namespace ExternalLib
{
    internal class StringCalculatorExternal
    {
        public string Num1 { get; set; }
        public string Num2 { get; set; }
    }
}
```

The code belongs to the assembly `ExternalLib` that contains a `StringCalculatorExternal` class of internal access modifiers with two properties, `Num1` and `Num2`, defined with the `public` access modifier. It will not work if we call this code from some other assembly. Let's consider the following code snippet:

```
namespace Day04
{
    internal class StringCalculator
    {
```

```
                 public int Sum()
                 {
                     //This will not work
                     StringCalculatorExternal externalLib = new
         StringCalculatorExternal();
                     return Convert.ToInt32(externalLib.Num1) +
         Convert.ToInt32(externalLib.Num2);
                 }
             }
         }
```

The preceding code is of a separate assembly day four, and we are trying to call a `StringCalculatorExternal` class of assembly `ExternalLib` that is not possible, as we have defined this class as `internal`. This code will throw the following error:

```
namespace Day04
{
    2 references | Gaurav Arora, 4 hours ago | 1 author, 2 changes
    internal class StringCalculator
    {


        1 reference | Gaurav Arora, 4 hours ago | 1 author, 1 change
        public int Sum()
        {
            //This will not work
            StringCalculatorExternal externalLib = new StringCalculatorExternal();
            return Convert.To                                                    .Num2);
        }                   'StringCalculatorExternal' is inaccessible due to its protection level
    }
}                           Cannot access internal class 'StringCalculatorExternal' here
```

composite

When we use protected and internal access modifier jointly i.e. protected internal this combinition of modifiers known as composite modifier.

 `protected internal` means protected or internal and not protected and internal. This means a member can be accessed from any class within the same assembly.

To understand protected internal accessibility levels, let's consider the following code example:

```
namespace Day04
{
    internal class StringCalculator
    {
        protected internal string Num1 { get; set; }
        protected internal string Num2 { get; set; }
    }

    internal class StringCalculatorImplement :
    StringCalculator
    {
        public int Sum() => Convert.ToInt32(Num1) + Convert.ToInt32(Num2);
    }
}
```

The preceding code is for assembly day four with a class `StringCalculatorImplement`, that is, the inherited `StringCalculator` class (this class has two properties with the `protected internal` access modifier). Let's consider code from the same assembly:

```
namespace Day04
{
    internal class Program
    {
        private static void Main(string[] args)
        {
            var calculator = new
            StringCalculatorImplement();
            Write("Enter number1:");
            calculator.Num1 = ReadLine();
            Write("Enter number2:");
            calculator.Num2 = ReadLine();


            Write($"Sum of {calculator.Num1} and
            {calculator.Num2} is {calculator.Sum()}");
            ReadLine();
        }
    }
}
```

The preceding code will produce the following output:

```
Example of protected internal
Enter number1:118
Enter number2:109
Sum of 118 and 109 is 227
```

private

A `private` modifier is the lowest scope of the member. This means whenever a member is defined using the `private` modifier, that member is only accessible within the class where it is defined.

 `private` means restricted access, and the member can only be accessed from within class or its nested types, if defined.

To understand private accessibility levels, let's consider the following code example:

```csharp
internal class StringCalculator
{
    private string Num1 { get; set; }
    private string Num2 { get; set; }

    public int Sum() => Convert.ToInt32(Num1) + Convert.ToInt32(Num2);
}
```

In the preceding code properties, `Num1` and `Num2` are not accessible to outside the `StringCalculator` class. The following code will not work:

```
internal class StringCalculatorAnother
{
    private readonly StringCalculator _calculator;

    public StringCalculatorAnother(StringCalculator
    calculator)
    {
        _calculator = calculator;
    }

    public int Sum() => Convert.ToInt32(_calculator.Num1) +
Convert.ToInt32(_calculator.Num2);
}
```

The preceding code will throw a compile-time error as in the following screenshot:

```
1 reference | 0 changes | 0 authors, 0 changes
internal class StringCalculatorAnother
{
    private readonly StringCalculator _calculator;

    0 references | 0 changes | 0 authors, 0 changes
    public StringCalculatorAnother(StringCalculator calculator)
    {
        _calculator = calculator;
    }

    0 references | 0 changes | 0 authors, 0 changes
    public int Sum()
    {
        return Convert.ToInt32(_calculator.Num1) + Convert.ToInt32(_calculator.Num2);
    }
}
```

'StringCalculator.Num1' is inaccessible due to its protection level

Cannot access private property 'Num1' here

Rules for the access modifier

We have discussed the access modifier and accessibility with the use of this access modifier. Now, there are certain rules we should follow while working with these access modifiers that are discussed here:

- **Combination restriction**: A restriction is there while using an access modifier. These modifiers should not be used in combination unless you are using access modifiers protected internal. Consider the code example discussed in the previous section.
- **Namespace restriction**: These access modifiers should not be used with namespace.
- **Default accessibility restriction**: When, or if, a member is declared without an access modifier, then default accessibility is used. All classes are implicitly internal, and its members are private.
- **Top-level type restriction**: Top-level types are parent types that have immediate parent type objects. Parent or top-level types cannot use any accessibility other than `internal` or `public` accessibility. If no access modifier is applied, default accessibility will be internal.
- **Nested-type restriction**: Nested types are those that are members of other types, or have immediate parent types other than universal types, that is, an object. The accessibility of these can be declared as discussed in the following table (`https:/ /docs.microsoft.com/en-us/dotnet/csharp/language-reference/keywords/ accessibility-levels`):

Nested Type	Default Accessibility for Members	Allowed Accessibility Can Be Declared	Description
Enum	`public`	None	`enum` has public accessibility, and its members have only `public` accessibility. These are meant to be used for other types; hence, they are not allowed to set any accessibility explicitly.

Class	private	public, internal, protected, private, protected internal	Class is internal by default, and members are `private`. Refer to the previous section-Rules for access modifier for more details.
Interface	public	None	Interface is internal by default, and its members are `public`. Members of interface are meant to be utilized from inherited types, so there is no explicit accessibility allowed for interface.
struct	private	public, internal, private	The same as `class`, struct is internal by default and its members are `private`. We can explicitly apply accessibility of `public`, `internal`, and `private`.

abstract

In simple words, we can say that an abstract modifier indicates that things are yet to be completed. A `class` is only meant to be a base class for other classes when an abstract modifier is used to create a `class`. Members marked as abstract in this `class` should be implemented in the derive class.

 The abstract modifier indicates incomplete things and can be used with class, method, property, indexer, and/or event. Members marked as abstract would not be allowed to define accessibility other than `public`, `protected`, `internal` and `protected internal`.

Abstract classes are half-defined. This means these provide a way to override members to child classes. We should use base classes in the project where we need to have the same member for all child classes with its own implementations or need to override. For example, let's consider an abstract class car with an abstract method color and have child classes Honda car, Ford car, Maruti car, and so on. In this case, all child classes would have color member but with different implementations because the color method would be overridden in the child classes with their own implementations. The point to be noted here is that abstract classes represent is-a relation.

To understand the capacity of this modifier, let's consider the following example:

```
namespace Day04
{
    internal abstract class StringCalculator
    {
        public abstract string Num1 { get; set; }
        protected abstract string Num2 { get; set; }
        internal abstract string Num3 { get; set; }
        protected internal abstract string Num4 { get;
        set; }

        public int Sum() => Convert.ToInt32(Num1) +
Convert.ToInt32(Num2);
    }
}
```

The preceding code snippet is an abstract class that contains abstract properties and a non-abstract method. Other classes can only implement this class. Please refer to the following code snippet:

```
internal class StringCalculatorImplement : StringCalculator
{
    public override string Num1 { get; set; }
    protected override string Num2 { get; set; }
    internal override string Num3 { get; set; }
    protected internal override string Num4 { get; set; }

    //other stuffs here
}
```

In the preceding code snippet, `StringCalculatorImplement` is implementing the abstract class `StringCalculator`, and all members are marked as abstract.

Rules of the abstract modifier

There are certain rules we need to follow while working with abstract modifiers, and these rules are discussed as follows:

- **Instantiation**: If a class is marked as abstract, we cannot create the instance of it. In other words, object initialization is not allowed for abstract classes. We will get a compile-time error if we try to do this explicitly. Refer to the following screenshot, where we are trying to instantiate an abstract class:

```
3 references | Gaurav Arora, 11 hours ago | 1 author, 3 changes
internal abstract class StringCalculator
{
    1 reference | Gaurav Arora, 11 hours ago | 1 author, 2 changes
    public abstract string Num1 { get; set; }
    1 reference | Gaurav Arora, 11 hours ago | 1 author, 2 changes
    protected abstract string Num2 { get; set; }

}

0 references | 0 changes | 0 authors, 0 changes
internal class StringCalculatorImplement : StringCalculator
{
    StringCalculator  calculator = new StringCalculator();
    1 reference | 0 changes | 0 authors, 0 changes
    public override string Num1 { get;       Cannot create an instance of the abstract class or interface 'StringCalculator'
    1 reference | 0 changes | 0 authors, 0 changes
    protected override string Num2 { g       Cannot create an instance of the abstract class 'Day04.StringCalculator'
}
```

- **Non-abstract**: A class may or may not contain abstract methods or members that are marked as abstract. This means there is no restriction when we have to create all abstract members and methods for abstract classes. The following code obeys this rule:

```csharp
internal abstract class StringCalculator
{
    public abstract string Num1 { get; set; }
    public abstract string Num2 { get; set; }
    public abstract int SumToBeImplement();

    //non-abstract
    public int Sum() => Convert.ToInt32(Num1) + Convert.ToInt32(Num2);
}


internal class StringCalculatorImplement : StringCalculator
{
```

```
    public override string Num1 { get; set; }
    public override string Num2 { get; set; }
    public override int SumToBeImplement() => Convert.ToInt32(Num1) +
Convert.ToInt32(Num2);
}
```

- **Limit-inherit nature**: As we discussed, an abstract class is meant to be inherited by other classes. If we do not want to inherit the abstract class from other classes, we should use a sealed modifier. We will discuss this in detail in the upcoming sections.

 For more information, refer to
https://docs.microsoft.com/en-us/dotnet/csharp/programming-guide
/classes-and-structs/abstract-and-sealed-classes-and-class-
members.

- **Implementation nature**: All members of an abstract class should be implemented in the child class that is inheriting the abstract class only if the child class is non-abstract. To understand this, let's consider the following examples:

```
internal abstract class StringCalculator
{
    public abstract string Num1 { get; set; }
    public abstract string Num2 { get; set; }
    public abstract int SumToBeImplement();

    //non-abstract
    public int Sum() => Convert.ToInt32(Num1) + Convert.ToInt32(Num2);
}
internal abstract class AnotherAbstractStringCalculator: StringCalculator
{
    //no need to implement members of StringCalculator class
}
```

The preceding code snippet is showing two abstract classes. A child abstract class, AnotherAbstractString, is inheriting another abstract class, StringCalculator. As both the classes are abstract, there's no need to implement members of the inherited abstract class that is StringCalculator.

Now, consider another example where the inherited class is non-abstract. In this case, the child class should implement all the abstract members of the abstract class; otherwise, it will throw a compile-time error. See the following screenshot:

```
1 reference | Gaurav Arora, 12 hours ago | 1 author, 3 changes
internal abstract class StringCalculator
{
    2 references | Gaurav Arora, 12 hours ago | 1 author, 2 changes
    public abstract string Num1 { get; set; }
    2 references | Gaurav Arora, 12 hours ago | 1 author, 2 changes
    public abstract string Num2 { get; set; }
    0 references | 0 changes | 0 authors, 0 changes
    public abstract int SumToBeImplement();

    //non-abstract
    0 references | Gaurav Arora, 20 hours ago | 1 author, 1 change
    public int Sum() => Convert.ToInt32(Num1) + Convert.ToInt32(Num2);
}
0 references | 0 changes | 0 authors, 0 changes
internal class StringCalculatorImplement : StringCalculator
{
    2 references | 0 changes | 0 authors, 0 changes
    public override string Num1 { get; set; }       class Day04.StringCalculator
    2 references | 0 changes | 0 authors, 0 changes
    public override string Num2 { get; set; }        Abstract inherited member 'int Day04.StringCalculator.SumToBeImplement()' is not implemented
    |
}
```

- **Virtual in nature**: Methods and properties marked as abstract for the abstract class are virtual, by default, in nature. These methods and properties will be overridden in inherited classes.

Here is the complete example of abstract class implementation:

```
internal abstract class StringCalculator
{
    public  string Num1 { get; set; }
    public  string Num2 { get; set; }
    public abstract int Sum();

}


internal class StringCalculatorImplement : StringCalculator
{
    public override int Sum() => Convert.ToInt32(Num1) +
Convert.ToInt32(Num2);
}
```

async

The `async` modifier provides a way to make a method of the anonymous type or a lambda expression as asynchronous. When it is used with a method, that method is called as the `async` method.

 `async` will be discussed in details on day six.

Consider the following code example:

```
internal class StringCalculator
{
    public string Num1 { get; set; }
    public string Num2 { get; set; }
    public async Task<int> Sum() => await
Task.Run(()=>Convert.ToInt32(Num1) +
        Convert.ToInt32(Num2));
}
```

The preceding code will provide the same result as discussed in the code examples in the previous sections; the only difference is this method call is asynchronous.

const

The `const` modifier gives the ability to define a constant field or constant local. When we defined fields or variables using `const`, these fields are not called variables anymore because `const` is not meant for change, while variables are. Constant fields are class-level constants that are accessible within or outside the `class` (depends upon their modifier), while constant locals are defined within a method.

 Fields and variables defined as `const` are not variables and may not be modified. These constants can be any of these: numbers, bool, string, or null references. A static modifier is not allowed while declaring constants.

Here is the code snippet that shows the valid constant declaration:

```
internal class StringCalculator
{
    private const int Num1 = 70;
    public const double Pi = 3.14;
    public const string Book = "Learn C# in 7-days";

    public int Sum()
    {
        const int num2 = Num1 + 85;
        return  Convert.ToInt32(Num1) + Convert.ToInt32(num2);
    }
}
```

event

The modifier `event` helps declare an event for the `publisher` class. We will discuss this in detail on day five. For more information on this modifier, refer to `https://docs.microsoft.com/en-us/dotnet/csharp/language-reference/keywords/event`.

extern

The modifier `extern` helps declare a method that uses an external library or dll. This is important when you want to use an external unmanaged library.

A method that is implementing external unmanaged libraries using the `extern` keyword must be declared as static. For more information, refer to `https://docs.microsoft.com/en-us/dotnet/csharp/language-reference/keywords/extern`.

new

The new operator can be a modifier, an operator, or modifier. Let's discuss this in detail:

- **Operator**: new as an operator helps us create an object instance of a class and invokes their constructors. For example, the following line is showing the use of new as an operator:

```
StringCalculator calculator = new StringCalculator();
```

- **Modifier**: The new modifier helps hide members inherited from a base class:

```
internal class StringCalculator
{
    private const int Num1 = 70;
    private const int Num2 = 89;

    public int Sum() => Num1 + Num2;
}


internal class StingCalculatorImplement : StringCalculator
{
    public int Num1 { get; set; }
    public int Num2 { get; set; }

    public new int Sum() => Num1 + Num2;
}
```

This is also known as hiding in C#.

- **Constraint**: The new operator as a constraint makes sure that in declaration of every generic class, it must have a public parameter-less constructor. This will be discussed in detail on day five.

override

The `override` modifier helps extend the abstract or virtual implementation of inherited members (that is, method, property, indexer, or event). This will be discussed in detail on day seven.

partial

With the help of the `partial` modifier, we can split a class, an interface, or a struct into multiple files. Look at the following code example:

```
namespace Day04
{
    public partial class Calculator
    {
        public int Add(int num1, int num2) => num1 + num2;
    }
}
namespace Day04
{
    public partial class Calculator
    {
        public int Sub(int num1, int num2) => num1 - num2;
    }
}
```

Here, we have two files, `Calculator.cs` and `Calculator1.cs`. Both files have `Calculator` as their partial class.

readonly

The `readonly` modifier helps us create a field declaration as `readonly`. A `readonly` field can only be assigned a value at the time of declaration or as part of the declaration itself. To understand this better, consider the following code snippet:

```
internal class StringCalculator
{
    private readonly int _num2;
    public readonly int Num1 = 179;

    public StringCalculator(int num2)
    {
```

```
        _num2 = num2;
    }

    public int Sum() => Num1 + _num2;
}
```

In the preceding code snippet, we have two fields, `Num1` and `_num2` are `readonly`. Here is the code snippet that tells us how to use these fields:

```
namespace Day04
{
    internal class Program
    {
        private static void Main(string[] args)
        {
            WriteLine("Example of readOnly modifier");
            Write("Enter number of your choice:");
            var num = ReadLine();
            StringCalculator calculator =
            newStringCalculator(Convert.ToInt32(num));
            Write($"Sum of {calculator.Num1} and {num} is
            {calculator.Sum()}");
            ReadLine();
        }
    }
}
```

In the preceding code-snippet, the field `_num2` is initialized from the constructor and `Num1` is initialized at the time of its declaration. When you run the preceding code, it generates output as shown in following screenshot:

```
Example of readOnly modifier
Enter number of your choice:505
Sum of 179 and 505 is 684
```

It will throw a compile-time error if we explicitly try to assign a value to the `Num1` `readonly` field. See the following screenshot:

```
namespace Day04
{
    0 references | Gaurav Arora, 18 hours ago | 1 author, 9 changes
    internal class Program
    {
        0 references | Gaurav Arora, 18 hours ago | 1 author, 6 changes
        private static void Main(string[] args)
        {
            WriteLine("Example of readOnly modifier");
            Write("Enter number of your choice:");
            var num = ReadLine();
            StringCalculator calculator = new StringCalculator(Convert.ToInt32(num));
            calculator.Num1 = 10;
            Write($"Sum o
            ReadLine();        A readonly field cannot be assigned to (except in a constructor or a variable initializer)
        }
                               Field 'Num1' is read-only (except in constructor). The assignment target must be an assignable variable, property or indexer
    }
}
```

In the code snippet shown in the preceding screenshot, we are trying to assign the value
`Num1` to the `readonly` field. This is not allowed, so it throws an error.

sealed

The modifier `sealed` is something that, when applied with a `class`, says, "I am not going
to be available for any kind of inheritance further. Do not inherit me now." In simple words,
this modifier restricts classes from being inherited by other classes.

> The modifier sealed is used with override when applying abstract
> methods (which are virtual in default by nature) to derived or inherited
> class.

To understand this better, let's consider the following code example:

```
internal abstract class StringCalculator
{
    public int Num1 { get; set; }
    public int Num2 { get; set; }


    public abstract int Sum();
    public virtual int Sub() => Num1 -Num2;
}
internal class Calc : StringCalculator
{
    public int Num3 { get; set; }
    public int Num4 { get; set; }
    public override int Sub() => Num3 - Num4;
    //This will not be inherited from within derive classes
```

```
        //any more
        public sealed override int Sum() => Num3 + Num4;
    }
```

The preceding code snippet is defining abstract class and its abstract method and a virtual method. Now, both abstract method and virtual method can be overridden in derived classes. So, in class `calc`, both the methods `Sum()` and `Sub()` are overridden. From here, method `Sub()` is available for further overriding, but `Sum()` is a sealed method, so we can't override this method anymore in derived classes. If we explicitly try to do this, it throws a compile-time error as shown in the following screenshot:

```
1 reference | 0 changes | 0 authors, 0 changes
internal class Calc : StringCalculator
{
    2 references | 0 changes | 0 authors, 0 changes
    public int Num3 { get; set; }
    2 references | 0 changes | 0 authors, 0 changes
    public int Num4 { get; set; }
    2 references | 0 changes | 0 authors, 0 changes
    public override int Sub() => Num3 - Num4;

    //This will not be inherited from within derive classes
    //any more
    3 references | 0 changes | 0 authors, 0 changes
    public sealed override int Sum() => Num3 + Num4;
}

0 references | 0 changes | 0 authors, 0 changes
internal sealed class SealedCalc : Calc
{
    2 references | 0 changes | 0 authors, 0 changes
    public override int Sub() => Num1 - Num2;

    3 references | 0 changes | 0 authors, 0 changes
    public override int Sum()
    {
                        Cannot override inherited method 'int Day04.Calc.Sum()' because it is sealed
    }
}
```

You cannot apply a sealed modifier on an abstract classes. If we explicitly try this, it eventually throws a compile-time error. See the following screenshot:

```
3 references | Gaurav Arora, 18 hours ago | 1 author, 7 changes
internal abstract class StringCalculator
{
    3 references | Gaurav Arora, 18 hours ago | 1 author, 5 changes
    public int Num1 { get; set; }
    1 reference | Gaurav Arora, 18 hours ago | 1 author, 5 changes
    public int Num2 { get; set; }

    1 reference | Gaurav Arora, 18 hours ago | 1 author, 5 changes
    public abstract int Sum();
    0 references | 0 changes | 0 authors, 0 changes
    public virtual int Sub() => Num1 -Num2;
}

0 references | 0 changes | 0 authors, 0 changes
internal abstract| sealed class Calc : StringCalculator
{
                                    'Calc': an abstract class cannot be sealed or static

                                    Class 'Day04.Calc' cannot be both abstract and sealed
}
```

static

The modifier `static` helps us declare static members. These members are actually also known as class-level members and not object-level members. This means there is no need to create an instance of object to use these members.

Rules for the static modifier

There are certain rules that need to be followed while working with the `static` modifier:

- **Restriction**: You can use the `static` modifier with only class, field, method, property, operator, event, and constructors. This modifier cannot be used with indexer and types other than `class`.
- **Nature by static**: When we declare a constant, it is implicitly static by nature. Consider the following code snippet:

```
internal class StringCalculator
{
    public const int Num1 = 10;
    public const int Num2 = 20;
}
```

The preceding `StringCalculator` class is has two constants, `Num1` and `Num2`. These are accessible by `class`, and there is no need to create an instance of `class`. See the following code snippet:

```
internal class Program
{
    private static void Main(string[] args)
    {
        WriteLine("Example of static modifier");
        Write($"Sum of {StringCalculator.Num1} and
        {StringCalculator.Num2} is{StringCalculator.Num1 +
        StringCalculator.Num2}");
        ReadLine();
    }
}
```

- **Complete static**: If class is defined with the use of the `static` modifier, then all the members of this `static` class should be `static`. There will be a compile-time error if a `static` class is explicitly defined to create non-static members. Consider the following screenshot:

```
4 references | Gaurav Arora, 20 hours ago | 1 author, 7 changes
internal static class StringCalculator
{
    public const int Num1 = 10;
    public const int Num2 = 20;

    0 references | Gaurav Arora, 20 hours ago | 1 author, 5 changes
    public static int Sum() => Num1 + Num2;
    0 references | 0 changes | 0 authors, 0 changes
    public int Sub() => Num1 - Num2;
}
```

'Sub': cannot declare instance members in a static class

Static class 'Day04.StringCalculator' cannot have non-static method 'int Sub()'

Show potential fixes (Ctrl+.)

- **Availability**: No need to create an instance of class to access the `static` member. The keyword `this` cannot be applied on `static` methods or properties. We have already discussed this, and base keywords, on day two.

unsafe

This modifier helps use unsafe code blocks. We will discuss this in detail on day six.

virtual

This modifier helps us define virtual methods that are meant to be overridden in inherited classes. See the following code:

```
internal class StringCalculator
{
    private const int Num1 = 70;
    private const int Num2 = 89;


    public virtual int Sum() => Num1 + Num2;
}


internal class StingCalculatorImplement : StringCalculator
{
    public int Num1 { get; set; }
    public int Num2 { get; set; }


    public override int Sum() => Num1 + Num2;
}
```

 For more information, refer to https://docs.microsoft.com/en-us/dotnet/csharp/language-reference/keywords/virtual.

Methods

A block of statements that have the access modifier, name, return type, and parameters (which may or may not be there) are nothing but a method. A method is meant to perform some tasks.

Methods are meant to call either by another method or by another program.

How to use a method?

As said earlier, methods are meant to perform some actions. So, any method or program that needs to utilize these actions could call/consume/use the defined method.

A method has various element discussed as follows:

- **Access modifier**: A method should have an access modifier (refer to the previous section for more details on modifier). The modifier helps us define the scope of method or the availability of the method, for example. A method defined using the `private` modifier can only be visible to its own class.
- **Return type**: After performing an action, a method may or may not return something. Method return type is based on the data types (refer to day two for information on datatypes). For example, if method is returning a number, its data type would be an int and its return type is `void` if the method does not return anything.
- **Name**: A name is unique within the `class`. Names are case sensitive. In the class `StringCalculator`, we cannot define two methods with the name `Sum()`.
- **Parameter(s):** These are optional for any method. This means a method may or may not have a parameter. Parameters are defined based on the datatype.
- **Functioning body**: A part of instructions to be executed by a method is nothing but a functionality of the method.

The following screenshot shows a typical method:

Before moving ahead, let's recall the requirements we discussed at the start of day four, where we created a method to calculate the sum of a string parameter list. Here is the program that meets these requirements:

```
namespace Day04
{
    class StringCalculatorUpdated
    {
        public int Add(string numbers)
        {
            int result=0;
            if (string.IsNullOrEmpty(numbers))
                return result;
            foreach (var n in numbers.Split(','))
            {
                result +=
                Convert.ToInt32(string.IsNullOrEmpty(n) ? "0" : n);
            }
            return result;
        }
    }
}
namespace Day04
{
    internal class Program
    {
        private static void Main(string[] args)
        {
            WriteLine("Example of method");
```

```
                    StringCalculatorUpdated calculator = new
                    StringCalculatorUpdated();
                    Write("Enter numbers comma separated:");
                    var num = ReadLine();
                    Write($"Sum of {num} is
                    {calculator.Add(num)}");
                    ReadLine();
                }
            }
        }
```

The preceding code produces output as expected. Refer to the following screenshot:

```
o This operation should only accept input in a string data type
o Add operation can take 0, 1, or 2 comma - separated numbers, and will return their sum for example "1" or "1, 2"
o Add operation should accept empty string but for an empty string it will return 0.

Enter numbers comma separated:
Sum of  is 0

Enter numbers comma separated:0,25,28,101,789,10054
Sum of 0,25,28,101,789,10054 is 10997
```

The preceding code is working absolutely fine but needs refactoring, so lets split our code into small methods:

```
namespace Day04
{
    internal class StringCalculatorUpdated
    {
        public int Add(string numbers) =>
        IsNullOrEmpty(numbers) ? 0 :
        AddStringNumbers(numbers);


        private bool IsNullOrEmpty(string numbers) =>
        string.IsNullOrEmpty(numbers);


        private int AddStringNumbers(string numbers) =>
        GetSplittedStrings(numbers).Sum(StringToInt32);

        private IEnumerable<string>
        GetSplittedStrings(string numbers) =>
        numbers.Split(',');
        private int StringToInt32(string n) =>
        Convert.ToInt32(string.IsNullOrEmpty(n) ? "0" : n);
    }
}
```

Code refactoring is beyond the scope of this book. For more details on code refactoring, refer to `https://www.packtpub.com/application-development/refactoring-microsoft-visual-studio-2010`.

Now, our code looks better and readable. This will produce the same output.

Properties

Properties are members of a class, structure, or interface generally called as a named member. The intended behaviors of properties are similar to fields with the difference being that the implementation of properties is possible with the use of accessors.

Properties are extensions to fields. The accessors get and set helps retrieve and assign value to property.

Here is the typical property (also called property with auto-property syntax) of a class:

```
public int Number { get; set; }
```

For auto property, compiler generates the backup field, which is nothing but a storage field. So, the preceding property would be shown as follows, with a backup field:

```
private int _number;

public int Number
{
    get { return _number; }
    set { _number = value; }
}
```

The preceding property with an expression body looks like this:

```
private int _number;
public int Number
{
    get => _number;
    set => _number = value;
}
```

For more details on the expression bodies property, refer to `https://visualstudiomagazine.com/articles/2015/06/03/c-sharp-6-expression-bodied-properties-dictionary-initializer.aspx`.

Types of properties

There are multiple flavors of properties we can declare or play. We just discussed auto properties and discussed how compiler converts it with a backup storage field. In this section, we will discuss the other types of properties available.

Read-write property

A property that allows us to store and retrieve values is nothing but a read-write property. A typical read-write property with backing storage field would have both `set` and `get` accessors. The `set` accessor stores the data of the data type of the property. Note that for the set accessor, there's always a single parameter, that is, value, and this matches the storage data or data type of the property.

Auto properties are automatically converted to property with backing storage fields by the compiler.

See the following code snippet to understand this in detail:

```
internal class ProeprtyExample
{
    private int _num1;
    //with backing field
    public int Num1
    {
        get => _num1;
        set => _num1 = value;
    }
    //auto property
    public int Num2 { get; set; }
}
```

Previously, we had two properties: one defined using the backing field and another by auto property. The accessor `set` is responsible for storing the data using the parameter value, and it matches the data type int, and `get` is responsible for retrieving the data of data type int.

Read-only property

A property defined with only the `get` accessor or with a private `set` accessor is called a read-only property.

 There is slight difference between read-only and `const`. Refer to `https://stackoverflow.com/questions/55984/what-is-the-difference-between-const-and-readonly` for more details.

As the name indicates, read-only properties only retrieve values. You cannot store the data in a read-only property. See the following code snippet for more details:

```
internal class PropertyExample
{
    public PropertyExample(int num1)
    {
        Num1 = num1;
    }
    //constructor restricted property
    public int Num1 { get; }
    //read-only auto proeprty
    public int Num2 { get; private set; }
    //read-only collection initialized property
    public IEnumerable<string> Numbers { get; } = new List<string>();
}
```

In the preceding code, we have three properties; all are read-only. `Num1` is a read-only property, and this is restricted by a constructor. This means you can set a property in a constructor only. `Num2` is a pure read-only property; this means it is meant to retrieve the data. Numbers is the auto-initializer read-only property; it has a default initialization for a property of collection.

Computed property

A property that returns the results of an expression is called a computed property. The expression may be based on other properties of the same class or based on any valid expression with CLR-compliant data types (for data types, refer to day two) that should be the same as the property data type.

 Computed properties return the results of an expression and cannot allow to set data, so these are some kind of read-only property.

To understand this in detail, let's consider the following:

Block-bodied members

In the block-bodied computed property, calculations are returned with the get accessor. Refer to the following example:

```
internal class ProeprtyExample
{
    //other stuff removed
    public int Num3 { get; set; }
    public int Num4 { get; set; }
    public int Sum {
        get
        {
            return Num3 + Num4;
        }
    }
}
```

In the preceding code, we have three properties: Num3, Num4 and Sum. The property Sum is a computed property that returns an expression result from within the get accessor.

Expression-bodied members

In expression-bodied, the computed property calculations are returned using lambda expression, which is used by the expression-bodied members. Refer to the following example:

```
internal class ProeprtyExample
{
    public int Num3 { get; set; }
    public int Num4 { get; set; }
```

```
    public int Add => Num3 + Num4;
}
```

In the preceding code, our `Add` property is returning an expression of `Sum` for two other properties.

Property using validation

There may be scenarios when we want to validate certain data for properties. Then, we would use a few validations along with properties. These are not a special type of property, but complete properties with validation.

Data annotation is a way to validate various properties and add custom validations. For more information, refer to `https://www.codeproject.com/Articles/826304/Basic-Introduction-to-Data-Annotation-in-NET-Frame`.

These properties are important in a scenario when we need to validate the input using properties. Consider the following code snippet:

```
internal class ProeprtyExample
{
    private int _number;
    public int Number
    {
        get => _number;
        set
        {
            if (value < 0)
            {
                //log for records or take action
                //Log("Number is negative.");
                throw new ArgumentException("Number can't be -ve.");
            }
            _number = value;
        }
    }
}
```

In the preceding code, there is no need to apply any explicit validation on the client code for the preceding property. The property `Number` is self-validated whenever it is being called to store data. In the previous code, whenever the client code tries to enter any negative number, it implicitly throws out an exception that the number can't be negative. In this case, only positive numbers are entered by the client code. On the same node, you can apply as much as validation as you want.

Indexers

An indexer provides a way to access an object via an index like array. For instance, if we define an indexer for a class, that class works similarly to an array. This means the collection of this class can be accessed by index.

 Keyword `this` is used to define an indexer. The main benefit of indexer is that we can set or retrieve the indexed value without explicitly specifying a type.

Consider the following code snippet:

```
public class PersonCollection
{
    private readonly string[] _persons = Persons();
    public bool this[string name] => IsValidPerson(name);
    private bool IsValidPerson(string name) =>
    _persons.Any(person => person == name);


    private static string[] Persons() => new[]
    {"Shivprasad","Denim","Vikas","Merint","Gaurav"};
}
```

The preceding code is a simpler one to represent the power of an indexer. We have a `PersonCollection` class having an indexer that makes this class accessible via indexer. Please refer to the following code:

```
private static void IndexerExample()
{
    WriteLine("Indexer example.");
    Write("Enter person name to search from collection:");
    var name = ReadLine();
    var person = new PersonCollection();
    var result = person[name] ? "exists." : "does not
    exist.";
    WriteLine($"Person name {name} {result}");
}
```

We can see the following output after executing the preceding code:

```
Indexer example.
Enter person name to search from collection:Shivprasad
Person name 'Shivprasad' exists.
```

For more information on indexers, refer to https://docs.microsoft.com/en-us/dotnet/csharp/programming-guide/indexers/.

File I/O

File is nothing but a collection of data that stores physically in a directory of the system. The data that file contains could be any information. In C#, whenever the file is available programmatically for information retrieval (read) or updating information (write), that is nothing but a stream.

 Stream is nothing but a sequence of bytes.

In the C# file, I/O is just a way to call input streams or output streams:

- **Input stream**: This is nothing but a read operation. Whenever we programmatically read the data from the file, it is called an input stream or a read operation.
- **Output stream**: This is nothing but an update operation. Whenever we programmatically add data to the file, it is called an output stream or a write operation.

File I/O is a part of the System.IO namespace that contains various classes. In this section, we will discuss FileStream that we will use in our code example.

 A complete list of System.IO classes is available at https://docs.microsoft.com/en-us/dotnet/api/system.io?view=netcore-2.0.

FileStream

As discussed previously, there are a couple of helpful classes that are available under the `System.IO` namespace. FileStream is one of these classes that helps us read/write data to/from a file. Before going on to discuss this `class`, let's consider one short example where we will create a file:

```
private static void FileInputOutputOperation()
{
    const string textLine = "This file is created during
    practice of C#";
    Write("Enter file name (without extension):");
    var fileName = ReadLine();
    var fileNameWithPath = $"D:/{fileName}.txt";
    using (var fileStream = File.Create(fileNameWithPath))
    {
        var iBytes = new
        UTF8Encoding(true).GetBytes(textLine);
        fileStream.Write(iBytes, 0, iBytes.Length);
    }
    WriteLine("Write operation is completed.");
    ReadLine();
    using (var fileStream =
    File.OpenRead(fileNameWithPath))
    {
        var bytes = new byte[1024];
        var encoding = new UTF8Encoding(true);
        while (fileStream.Read(bytes, 0, bytes.Length) >
        0)
        WriteLine(encoding.GetString(bytes));
    }
}
```

The preceding code first creates a file with specific text/data and then displays the same. Here is the output of the preceding code. Refer to the following screenshot:

```
Enter file name (without extension):help
Write operation is completed.

This file is created during practice of C#
```

A complete reference of FileStream is available at
`https://docs.microsoft.com/en-us/dotnet/api/system.io.filestream`
`?view=netcore-2.0`.

Exception handling

Exception is a kind of error that comes when methods do not work as expected or are not able to handle the situation as intended. Sometimes, there might be unknown situations where exceptions occurred; for instance, a method can have a situation divide by zero problem in division operation the situation was never expected while someone wrote the method, this is an unpredicted situational error. To handle these kind of situations and other unknown scenarios that can create such exceptions or error, C# provides a method that is called exception handling. In this section, we will discuss exceptions and exception handing using C# in details.

Exceptions can be handled using the `try...catch...finally` block. Catch or finally blocks should be there with the try block to handle exceptions.

Consider the following code:

```
class ExceptionhandlingExample
    {
        public int Div(int dividend,int divisor)
        {
            //thrown an exception if divisor is 0
            return dividend / divisor;
        }
    }
```

The preceding code will throw an unhandled divide by zero exception if the divisor comes as zero once called using the following code:

```
private static void ExceptionExample()
{
    WriteLine("Exaception handling example.");
    ExceptionhandlingExample example = new ExceptionhandlingExample();
    Write("Enter dividen:");
    var dividend = ReadLine();
    Write("Enter divisor:");
    var divisor = ReadLine();
    var quotient = example.Div(Convert.ToInt32(dividend),
```

```
Convert.ToInt32(divisor));
    WriteLine($"Quotient of dividend:{dividend}, divisio:{divisor} is
{quotient}");
}
```

See the following screenshot for the exception:

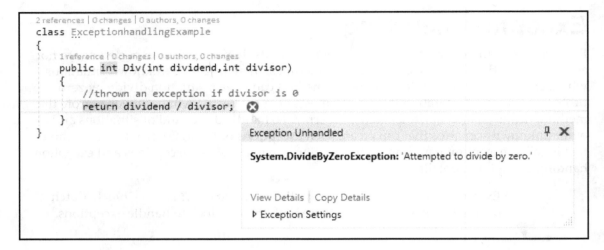

To handle situations similar to the previous situation, we can use exception handling. In C#, exception handling has common components, which are discussed here.

try block

The try block is a code of block that is the source of the exception. A try block can have multiple catch blocks and/or one final bock. This means a try block should have at least one catch block or one final block.

catch block

The catch block is a code block where a particular or general exception is being handled. The catch has a parameter of Exception that tells us what exception has occurred.

finally block

A `finally` block is one that executes in any case (if supplied) whether an exception is thrown or not. Generally, a `finally` block is meant to execute few cleanup tasks after exception.

  The `throw` keyword helps to throw a system or a custom exception.

Now, let's revisit the preceding code that threw an exception:

```
class ExceptionhandlingExample
{
    public int Div(int dividend,int divisor)
    {
        int quotient = 0;
        try
        {
            quotient = dividend / divisor;
        }
        catch (Exception exception)
        {
            Console.WriteLine($"Exception occuered
            '{exception.Message}'");
        }
        finally
        {
            Console.WriteLine("Exception occured and cleaned.");
        }
        return quotient;
    }
}
```

Here, we have modified the code by adding `try...catch...finally` blocks. Now, whenever an exception occurs, it first goes to the `catch` block and then to the `finally` block. After putting the `finally` block, whenever we divide by zero an exception will occur, which will produce the following result:

```
Exaception handling example.
Enter dividen:1
Enter divisor:0
Exception occuered 'Attempted to divide by zero.'
Exception occured and cleaned.
Quotient of dividend:1, divisio:0 is 0
```

Different compiler-generated exceptions in catch block

As we discussed previously, there may be multiple `catch` blocks within a `try` block. This means we can catch multiple exceptions. The different `catch` block could be written to handle a specific exception class. For example, an `exception` class for divide by zero exception is `System.DivideByZeroException`. A complete discussion of all these classes is beyond the scope of this book. For further study on these exception classes, refer to `https://docs.microsoft.com/en-us/dotnet/csharp/programming-guide/exceptions/compiler-generated-exceptions`.

User-defined exceptions

Custom exceptions created as per requirements are user exceptions, and when we create an `exception` class, to handle a specific scenario, it is called a user-defined exception. All user-defined `exception` classes are derived from the `Exception` class.

Let's create a user-defined `exception`. Recall the `StringCalculatorUpdated` class (discussed in the section **Methods**) that is responsible for calculating the sum of string numbers. Add one more scenario to the existing requirements, that is, throw the `NumberIsExceded` exception if any number is greater than 1,000:

```
internal class NumberIsExcededException : Exception
{
    public NumberIsExcededException(string message) :
    base(message)
    {
    }
    public NumberIsExcededException(string message,
```

```
Exception innerException):base(message,innerException)
{
}
protected NumberIsExcededException(SerializationInfo
serializationInfo, StreamingContext streamingContext)
: base(serializationInfo, streamingContext) {}
}
```

The preceding code snippet represents our NumberIsExcededException class. We have three constructors and all are self-explanatory. The third constructor is for serialization. If required here, we can do the serialization. So, when the exception goes to client from the remote server, it should be serialized.

Here is the code snippet that handles our newly created exception:

```
internal class StringCalculatorUpdated
{
    public int Add(string numbers)
    {
        var result = 0;
        try
        {
            return IsNullOrEmpty(numbers) ? result :
            AddStringNumbers(numbers);
        }
        catch (NumberIsExcededException excededException)
        {
            Console.WriteLine($"Exception
            occurred:'{excededException.Message}'");
        }

        return result;
    }
    //other stuffs omitted

    private int StringToInt32(string n)
    {
        var number =
        Convert.ToInt32(string.IsNullOrEmpty(n) ? "0" : n);
        if(number>1000)
            throw new NumberIsExcededException($"Number
            :{number} excedes the limit of 1000.");
        return number;
    }
}
```

Now, whenever the number exceeds 1,000, it throws an exception. Let's write a client code that throws an exception, consider the preceding code is called:

```
private static void CallStringCalculatorUpdated()
{
    WriteLine("Rules for operation:");
    WriteLine("o This operation should only accept input
    in a string data type\n" +
            "o Add operation can take 0, 1, or 2 comma -
            separated numbers, and will return their sum
            for example \"1\" or \"1, 2\"\n" +
            "o Add operation should accept empty string
            but for an empty string it will return 0.\n"
            +
            "o Throw an exception if number > 1000\n");
            StringCalculatorUpdated calculator = new
            StringCalculatorUpdated();
    Write("Enter numbers comma separated:");
    var num = ReadLine();


    Write($"Sum of {num} is {calculator.Add(num)}");
}
```

The preceding code will generate the following output:

```
Rules for operation:
o This operation should only accept input in a string data type
o Add operation can take 0, 1, or 2 comma - separated numbers, and will return their sum for example "1" or "1, 2"
o Add operation should accept empty string but for an empty string it will return 0.
o Throw an exception if number > 1000

Enter numbers comma separated:15,19,1005
Exception occurred:'Number:1005 excedes the limit of 1000.'
Sum of 15,19,1005 is 0
```

Discussing a regular expression and its importance

A regular expression or pattern matching is nothing but a way in which we can check whether an input string is correct or not. This is possible with the use of the Regex class of the System.Text.RegularExpressions namespace.

The Importance of a regular expression

Pattern matching is very important while we are working to validate text input. Here, regular expression plays an important role.

Flexible

Patterns are very flexible and provide us with a way to make our own pattern to validate the input.

Constructs

There are various constructs that help us define the regular expression. Hence, we need to make them important in our programming where we need validated input. These constructs are character classes, character escapes, quantifiers, and so on.

Special characters

There is a huge usage of regular expressions in our day-to-day programmings and that why regular expressions are important. Here are various scenarios as per their usage, where special characters of regular expression helps us validate the input when it comes with a pattern.

The period sign (.)

This is a wildcard character that matches any character besides the newline character.

The word sign (w)

Backslash and a lowercase *w* is a character class that will match any word character.

The space sign (s)

White space can be matched using *s* (backslash and *s*).

The digit sign (d)

The digits zero to nine can be matched using *d* (backslash and lowercase *d*).

The hyphen sign (-)

Ranges of characters can be matched using the hyphen (-).

Specifying the number of matches

The minimum number of matches required for a character, group, or character class can be specified with curly brackets (*{n}*).

Here is the code snippet showing the previous special characters:

```
private static void ValidateInputText(string inputText, string regExp,bool
isCllection=false,RegexOptions option=RegexOptions.IgnoreCase)
{
    var regularExp = new Regex(regExp,option);


    if (isCllection)
    {
        var matches = regularExp.Matches(inputText);
        foreach (var match in matches)
        {
            WriteLine($"Text '{inputText}' matches
            '{match}' with pattern'{regExp}'");
        }
    }
    var singleMatch = Regex.Match(inputText, regExp,
    option);
    WriteLine($"Text '{inputText}' matches '{singleMatch}'
    with pattern '{regExp}'");
    ReadLine();


}
```

The preceding code allows `inputText` and `Regexpression` to be performed on it. Here is the calling code:

```
private static void RegularExpressionExample()
{
    WriteLine("Regular expression example.\n");
    Write("Enter input text to match:");
    var inpuText = ReadLine();
    if (string.IsNullOrEmpty(inpuText))
        inpuText = @"The quick brown fox jumps over the lazy dog.";
    WriteLine("Following is the match based on different pattern:\n");
    const string theDot = @"\.";
```

```
    WriteLine("The Period sign [.]");
    ValidateInputText(inpuText,theDot,true);
    const string theword = @"\w";
    WriteLine("The Word sign [w]");
    ValidateInputText(inpuText, theword, true);
    const string theSpace = @"\s";
    WriteLine("The Space sign [s]");
    ValidateInputText(inpuText, theSpace, true);
    const string theSquareBracket = @"\[The]";
    WriteLine("The Square-Brackets sign [( )]");
    ValidateInputText(inpuText, theSquareBracket, true);
    const string theHyphen = @"\[a-z0-9]ww";
    WriteLine("The Hyphen sign [-]");
    ValidateInputText(inpuText, theHyphen, true);
    const string theStar = @"\[a*]";
    WriteLine("The Star sign [*] ");
    ValidateInputText(inpuText, theStar, true);
    const string thePlus = @"\[a+]";
    WriteLine("The Plus sign [+] ");
    ValidateInputText(inpuText, thePlus, true);
}
```

The preceding code generates the following output:

Regular expression is a broad topic. For more details, refer to `https://docs.microsoft.com/en-us/dotnet/api/system.text.regularexpressions?view=netcore-2.0`.

Hands-on exercise

Here are the unsolved questions from what you learned up until day four:

1. What are access modifiers and their accessibility?
2. Write a program to use `protected internal`.
3. What are abstract classes? Elaborate with the help of a program.
4. Does an abstract class have a constructor? If yes, the why can't we instantiate abstract class? (Refer to `https://stackoverflow.com/questions/2700256/why-cant-an-object-of-abstract-class-be-created`)
5. Explain, with the help of a small program, how we can stop an abstract class from being inherited.
6. Differentiate the `sync` and `async` methods.
7. Differentiate the `const` and `readOnly` modifiers with the help of a small program.
8. Write a program to calculate string numbers in addition to the following rules to our `StringCalcuatorUpdated` example:

   - Throw an exception where the number is greater than 1,000.
   - Ignore negative numbers by replacing them with zero.
   - If the entered string is not a number, throw an exception.

9. Write a small program to elaborate on property types.
10. Create a property using validation to meet all rules discussed in *question 8*.
11. What is an exception?
12. How we can handle exceptions in C#? Elaborate using a small program.
13. Write a user-defined exception if a string contains special characters other than delimiters, as defined in the requirements of our class `StringCalculatorUpdated`.

14. Write a program to create a file dynamically with the use of various classes of the `System.IO` namespace (refer to `https://docs.microsoft.com/en-us/dotnet/api/system.io.filestream?view=netcore-2.0`).

15. What are indexers? Write a short program to create a collection of paginated list.

16. What are regular expressions and how are they helpful in string manipulation. Elaborate using a small program.

Revisiting Day 04

We are concluding our day four learning. Today, we discussed all available modifiers and went through the code examples of these modifiers; we also discussed accessor modifiers, namely `public`, `private`, `internal`, `protected`, and so on.

Then, we came to methods and properties, where we discussed various scenarios and dealt with programs. We also discussed the indexer and file I/O, and we concluded our day by learning regular expressions. We went through the constants and we discussed constant filed and constant local.

Tomorrow, that is, on day five, we will discuss some advanced concepts covering reflection and understand how we can create and execute code dynamically.

Day 05 - Overview of Reflection and Collections

Today is day five of our seven-day learning series. Up till now, we have gone through various insights into the C# language and have got the idea about how to work with statements, loops, methods, and so on. Today, we will learn the best way to work dynamically when we're writing code.

There are lots of ways we can dynamically implement code changes and generate an entire programming class. Today, we will cover the following topics:

- What is reflection?
- Overview of delegates and events
- Collections and non-generics

What is reflection?

In simple terms, reflection is a way to get inside of a program, gathering the object information of a program/code and/or invoking these at runtime. So, with the help of reflection, we can analyze and assess our code by writing code in C#. To understand reflection in detail, let's take the example of the `class OddEven`. Here is the partial code of this class:

```
public class OddEven
{
    public string PrintOddEven(int startNumber, int
    lastNumber)
    {
      return GetOddEvenWithinRange(startNumber,
```

```
        lastNumber);
    }
    public string PrintSingleOddEven(int number) =>
CheckSingleNumberOddEvenPrimeResult(number);
    private string CheckSingleNumberOddEvenPrimeResult(int
    number)
    {
        var result = string.Empty;
        result = CheckSingleNumberOddEvenPrimeResult(result,
        number);
        return result;
    }
    //Rest code is omitted
}
```

After going through the code, we can say this code has a few public methods and private methods. Public methods utilize private methods for various functional demands and perform tasks to solve a real-world problems where we need to identify the odd or even numbers.

When we need to utilize the preceding class, we have to instantiate this class and then call their methods to get the results. Here is how we can utilize this simple class to get the results:

```
class Program
{
    static void Main(string[] args)
    {
        int userInput;
        do
        {
            userInput = DisplayMenu();
            switch (userInput)
            {
                case 1:
                Console.Clear();
                Console.Write("Enter number: ");
                var number = Console.ReadLine();
                var objectOddEven = new OddEven();
                var result =
                objectOddEven.PrintSingleOddEven
                (Convert.ToInt32(number));
                Console.WriteLine
                ($"Number:{number} is {result}");
                PressAnyKey();
                break;
                //Rest code is omitted
```

```
            } while (userInput != 3);
        }
    //Rest code is ommitted
}
```

In the preceding code snippet, we are just accepting an input from a user as a single number and then creating an object of our class, so we can call the method `PrintSingleOddEven` to check whether an entered number is odd or even. The following screenshot shows the output of our implementation:

```
Example - Day05

1. Find Odd Even without reflection.
2. Find Odd Even using reflection
3. Exit
Enter choice (1-3): 1

Enter number: 9
Number:9 is Odd
Press any key...
```

The previous code shows one of the ways in which we can implement the code. In the same way, we can implement this using the same solution but by analyzing the code. We have already stated that reflection is a way to analyse our code. In the upcoming section, we will implement and discuss the code of a similar implementation, but with the use of reflection.

 You need to add the following NuGet package to work with reflection, using the Package Manager Console: install-`Package` `System.Reflection`.

In the following code snippet, we will implement what we did in our previous code snippet, but here we will use `Reflection` to solve the same problem and achieve the same results:

```
class Program
{
    private static void Main(string[] args)
    {
        int userInput;
        do
        {
            userInput = DisplayMenu();
            switch (userInput)
            {
```

```
                    //Code omitted
                    case 2:
                    Console.Clear();
                    Console.Write("Enter number: ");
                    var num = Console.ReadLine();
                    Object objInstance =
                    Activator.CreateInstance(typeof(OddEven));
                    MethodInfo method =
                    typeof(OddEven).GetMethod
                    ("PrintSingleOddEven");
                    object res = method.Invoke
                    (objInstance, new object[]
                    { Convert.ToInt32(num) });
                    Console.WriteLine($"Number:{num} is {res}");
                    PressAnyKey();
                    break;
                }
          } while (userInput != 3);
        }
      //code omitted
  }
```

The preceding code snippet is simple to define: here, we are getting `MethodInfo` with the use of `System.Reflection` and thereafter invoking the method by passing the required parameters. The preceding example is the simplest one to showcase the power of `Reflection`; we can do more things with the use of `Reflection`.

In the preceding code, instead of `Activator.CreateInstance(typeof(OddEven))`, we can also use `Assembly.CreateInstance("OddEven")`. `Assembly.CreateInstance` looks into the type of the assembly and creates the instance using `Activator.CreateInstance`. For more information on `Assembly,CreateInstance`, refer to: `https://docs.microsoft.com/en-us/dotnet/api/system.reflection.assembly.createinstance?view=netstandard-2.0#System_Reflection_Assembly_CreateInstance_System_String_`.

Here is the output from the preceding code:

```
Example - Day05

1. Find Odd Even without reflection.
2. Find Odd Even using reflection
3. Exit
Enter choice (1-3): 2

Enter number: 9
Number:9 is Odd
Press any key...
```

Reflection in use

In the previous section, we get an idea about reflection and how we can utilize the power of Reflection to analyse the code. In this section, we will see more complex scenarios where we can use Reflection and discuss System.Type and System.Reflection in more detail.

Getting type info

There is a System.Type class available which provides us with the complete information about our object type: we can use typeof to get all the information about our class. Let's see the following code snippet:

```
class Program
{
    private static void Main(string[] args)
    {
        int userInput;
        do
        {
            userInput = DisplayMenu();
            switch (userInput)
            {
                // code omitted
                case 3:
                Console.Clear();
                Console.WriteLine
                ("Getting information using 'typeof' operator
                for class 'Day05.Program");
                var typeInfo = typeof(Program);
```

```
            Console.WriteLine();
            Console.WriteLine("Analysis result(s):");
            Console.WriteLine
            ("==========================");
            Console.WriteLine($"Assembly:
            {typeInfo.AssemblyQualifiedName}");
            Console.WriteLine($"Name:{typeInfo.Name}");
            Console.WriteLine($"Full Name:
            {typeInfo.FullName}");
            Console.WriteLine($"Namespace:
            {typeInfo.Namespace}");
            Console.WriteLine
            ("==========================");
            PressAnyKey();
            break;
            code omitted
        }
    } while (userInput != 5);
}
    //code omitted
}
```

In the previous code snippet, we used `typeof` to gather the information on our `class Program`. The `typeof` operator represents a type declaration here; in our case, it is a type declaration of `class Program`. Here is the result of the preceding code:

```
Getting information using 'typeof' operator for class 'Day05.Program'

Analysis result(s):
==========================
Assembly:Day05.Program, Day05, Version=1.0.0.0, Culture=neutral, PublicKeyToken=null
Name:Program
Full Name:Day05.Program
Namespace:Day05
==========================
Press any key...
```

On the same node, we can we have method `GetType()` of the `System.Type` class, which gets the type and provides the information. Let us analyse and discuss the following code snippet:

```
internal class Program
{
    private static void Main(string[] args)
    {
        int userInput;
        do
```

```
    {
        userInput = DisplayMenu();
        switch (userInput)
        {
            //code omitted
            case 4:
            Console.Clear();
            Console.WriteLine("Getting information using
            'GetType()' method for class
            'Day05.Program'");
            var info = Type.GetType("Day05.Program");
            Console.WriteLine();
            Console.WriteLine("Analysis result(s):");
            Console.WriteLine
            ("=========================");
            Console.WriteLine($"Assembly:
            {info.AssemblyQualifiedName}");
            Console.WriteLine($"Name:{info.Name}");
            Console.WriteLine($"Full Name:
            {info.FullName}");
            Console.WriteLine($"Namespace:
            {info.Namespace}");
            Console.WriteLine
            ("=========================");
            PressAnyKey();
            break;
        }
    } while (userInput != 5);
    }
    //code omitted
}
```

In the previous code snippet, we are gathering all information on `class Program` with the use of `GetMethod()`, and it results in the following:

```
Getting information using 'GetType()' method for class 'Day05.Program'

Analysis result(s):
=========================
Assembly:Day05.Program, Day05, Version=1.0.0.0, Culture=neutral, PublicKeyToken=null
Name:Program
Full Name:Day05.Program
Namespace:Day05
=========================
Press any key...
```

The code snippets discussed in the previous sections had a type which represented a class `System.Type`, and then we gathered the information using properties. These properties are explained in the following table:

Property name	Description
Name	Returns the name of the type, for example, `Program`
Full Name	Returns the fully qualified name of the type without the assembly name, for example, `Day05.Program`
Namespace	Returns the namespace of the type, for example, `Day05`. This property returns null if there is no namespace

These properties are read-only (of class `System.Type` which is an abstract class); that means we can only read or get the results, but they do not allow us to set the values.

 The `System.Reflection.TypeExtensions` class has everything we need to analyse and write code dynamically. The complete source code is available at `https://github.com/dotnet/corefx/blob/master/src/System.Reflection.TypeExtensions/src/System/Reflection/TypeExtensions.cs`.

Implementation of all extension methods is beyond the scope of this book, so we added the following table which represents all details on important extension methods:

Method name	Description	Source (`https://github.com/dotnet/corefx/blob/master/src`)
`GetConstructor(Type type, Type[] types)`	Performs over the provided type and returns output of type `System.Reflection.ConstructorInfo`	`/System.Reflection.Emit/ref/System.Reflection.Emit.cs`
`ConstructorInfo[] GetConstructors(Type type)`	Returns all constructor information for provided type and array outputs of `System.Reflection.ConstructorInfo`	`/System.Reflection.Emit/ref/System.Reflection.Emit.cs`
`ConstructorInfo[] GetConstructors(Type type, BindingFlags bindingAttr)`	Returns all constructor information for provided type and attributes	`/System.Reflection.Emit/ref/System.Reflection.Emit.cs`

MemberInfo[] GetDefaultMembers(Type type)	Gets the access for provided attribute, for member, for given type, and for outputs of array `System.Reflection.MemberInfo`	`/System.Reflection.Emit/ref/System.Reflection.Emit.cs`
EventInfo GetEvent(Type type, string name)	Provides the access to EventMetadata outputs of `System.Reflection.MemberInfo`	`/System.Reflection.Emit/ref/System.Reflection.Emit.cs`
FieldInfo GetField(Type type, string name)	Gets the field info of the specified type, and for the field name provided, and returns, output of `System.Reflection.FieldInfo`	`/System.Reflection.Emit/ref/System.Reflection.Emit.cs`
MemberInfo[] GetMember(Type type, string name)	Gets the member info of the specified type by using member name, and this method outputs an array of `System.Reflection.MemberInfo`	`/System.Reflection.Emit/ref/System.Reflection.Emit.cs`
PropertyInfo[] GetProperties(Type type)	Provides all properties for the specified type and outputs as an array of `System.Reflection.PropertyInfo`	`/System.Reflection.Emit/ref/System.Reflection.Emit.cs`

 Try implementing all extension methods using a simple program.

In previous sections, we learned how to analyze our compiled code/application using `Reflection`. `Reflection` works fine when we have existing code. Think of a scenario where we require some dynamic code generation logic. Let's say we need to generate a simple class as mentioned in following code snippet:

```
public class MathClass
{
    private readonly int _num1;
    private readonly int _num2;
    public MathClass(int num1, int num2)
    {
        _num1 = num1;
```

```
        _num2 = num2;
    }
    public int Sum() => _num1 + _num2;
    public int Substract() => _num1 - _num2;
    public int Division() => _num1 / _num2;
    public int Mod() => _num1 % _num2;
}
```

Creating or writing purely dynamic code or code on the fly is not possible with the sole use of `Reflection`. With the help of `Reflection`, we can analyze our `MathClass`, but we can create this class on the fly with the use of `Reflection.Emit`.

 Dynamic code generation is beyond the scope of this book. You can refer to the following thread for more information:
https://stackoverflow.com/questions/41784393/how-to-emit-a-type-in-net-core

Overview of delegates and events

In this section, we will discuss the basics of delegates and events. Both delegates and events are the most advanced features of the C# language. We will understand these in coming sections in detail.

Delegates

In C#, delegates are a similar concept to pointers to functions, as in C and C++. A delegate is nothing but a variable of a reference type, which holds a reference of a method, and this method is triggered.

 We can achieve late binding using delegates. In Chapter 7, *Understanding Object Oriented Programing with C#*, we will discuss late binding in detail.

`System.Delegate` is a class from which all delegates are derived. We use delegates to implement events.

Declaring a delegate type

Declaring a delegate type is similar to the method signature class. We just need to declare a type public delegate string: `PrintFizzBuzz(int number);`. In the preceding code, we declared a delegate type. This declaration is similar to an abstract method with the difference that delegate declaration has a type delegate. We just declared a delegate type `PrintFizzBuzz`, and it accepts one argument of int type and returns the result of the string. We can only declare public or internal accessible delegates.

 Accessibility of delegates is internal by default.

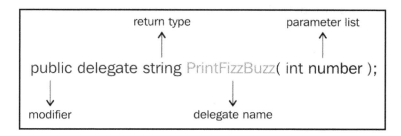

In the previous figure, we can analyse the syntax of the delegate declaration. If we saw this figure, we would notice that it started with public, then the keyword delegate, which tells us that this is a delegate type, the string, which is a return type, and our syntax is concluded with name and passing arguments. The following table defines that declaration has major parts:

Syntax part	Description
Modifier	Modifier is the defined accessibility of a delegate type. These modifiers can be only public or internal, and by default a delegate type modifier is internal.
Return type	Delegate can or cannot return a result; it can be of any type or void.
Name	The name of the declared delegate. The name of the delegate type follows the same rules as a typical class, as discussed on day two.
Parameter list	A typical parameter list; parameters can be any type.

Instances of delegate

In the previous section, we created a delegate type named `PrintFizzBuzz`. Now we need to declare an instance of this type so we can use the same in our code. This is similar to the way we declared variables—please refer to day two to know more about the declaration of variables. The following code snippet tells us how we can declare an instance of our delegate type:

```
PrintFizzBuzz printFizzBuzz;
```

Delegates in use

We can directly use delegate types by calling matching methods, which means the delegate type invokes a related method. In the following code snippet, we are simply invoking a method:

```
internal class Program
{
    private static PrintFizzBuzz _printFizzBuzz;
    private static void Main(string[] args)
    {
        int userInput;
        do
        {
            userInput = DisplayMenu();
            switch (userInput)
            {
                //code omitted
                case 6:
                Clear();
                Write("Enter number: ");
                var inputNum = ReadLine();
                _printFizzBuzz = FizzBuzz.PrintFizzBuzz;
                WriteLine($"Entered number:{inputNum} is
                {_printFizzBuzz(Convert.ToInt32(inputNum))}");
                PressAnyKey();
                break;
            }
        } while (userInput != 7);
    }
```

In the code snippet written in the previous section, we are taking an input from the user and then, with the help of the delegate, we are getting the expected results. The following screenshot shows the complete output of the preceding code:

```
Example - Day05

1. Find Odd Even without reflection.
2. Find Odd Even using reflection.
3. Showing power of System.Type class - use typeof.
4. Showing power of System.Type class - use GetType().
5. Complete information using System.Reflection.Extensins class.
6. Delegates, Events Example
7. Exit
Enter choice (1-7): 6

Enter number: 15
Entered number:15 is FizzBuzz
Press any key...
```

More advanced delegates, namely multicast, and strongly typed delegates will be discussed on day six.

Events

In general, whenever events come into the picture, we can think about an action for the user or user action. There are a couple of examples from our daily life; namely we check our emails, send emails, and so on. Actions such as clicking a send button or receive button from our email clients are nothing but events.

Events are members of a type, and this type is of delegate type. These members notify to other types when raised.

Events use the publisher-subscriber model. A publisher is nothing but an object which has a definition of the event and the delegate. On the other hand, a subscriber is an object which accepts the events and provides the event handler (event handlers are nothing but a method which is invoked by delegates in the publisher class).

Declaring an event

Before we declare an event, we should have a delegate type, so we should first declare a delegate. The following code snippet shows delegate type:

```
public delegate string FizzBuzzDelegate(int num);
The following code snippet shows event declaration:
public event FizzBuzzDelegate FizzBuzzEvent;
The following code snippet shows a complete implementation of an event to
find FizzBuzz numbers:
public delegate string FizzBuzzDelegate(int num);
public class FizzBuzzImpl
{
    public FizzBuzzImpl()
    {
        FizzBuzzEvent += PrintFizzBuzz;
    }
        public event FizzBuzzDelegate FizzBuzzEvent;
        private string PrintFizzBuzz(int num) => FizzBuzz.PrintFizzBuzz(num);
        public string EventImplementation(int num)
    {
        var fizzBuzImpl = new FizzBuzzImpl();
        return fizzBuzImpl.FizzBuzzEvent(num);
    }
}
```

The code snippet written in the previous section defines how the event internally called the attached method of delegate type. Here, we have an event called `FizzBuzzEvent` that is attached to a delegate type named `FizzBuzzDelegate`, which called a method `PrintFizzBuzz` on instantiation of our class named `FizzBuzzImpl`. Hence, whenever we call our event `FizzBuzzEvent`, it automatically calls a method `PrintFizzBuzz` and returns the expected results:

```
Example - Day05

1. Find Odd Even without reflection.
2. Find Odd Even using reflection.
3. Showing power of System.Type class - use typeof.
4. Showing power of System.Type class - use GetType().
5. Complete information using System.Reflection.Extensins class.
6. Delegates, Events Example
7. Exit
Enter choice (1-7): 6

Enter number: 15
using delegate:
Entered number:15 is FizzBuzz

using event:
Entered number:15 is FizzBuzz
Press any key...
```

Collections and non-generics

On day two, we learned about arrays, which are of fixed size, and you can use these for strongly typed list objects. But what about if we want to use or organize these objects into other data structures such as queues, lists, stacks, and so on? All these we can achieve with the use of collections (`System.Collections`).

There are various ways to play with data (storage and retrieval) with the use of collections. The following are the main collection classes we can use.

System.Collections.NonGeneric (https://www.nuget.org/packages/System.Collections.NonGeneric/) is a NuGet package which provides all non-generic types, namely `ArrayList`, `HashTable`, `Stack`, `SortedList`, `Queue`, and so on.

ArrayList

As it is an array, it contains an ordered collection of an object and can be indexed individually. As this is a non-generic class, it is available under a separate NuGet package from `System.Collections.NonGeneric`. To work with the example code, you should first install this NuGet package.

Declaration of ArrayList

The declaring part is very simple: you can just define it as a variable of the `ArrayList` type. The following code snippet shows how we can declare `ArrayList`:

```
ArrayList arrayList = new ArrayList();
ArrayList arrayList1 = new ArrayList(capacity);
ArrayList arrayList2 = new ArrayList(collection);
```

In the preceding code snippet, `arrayList` is initialized using the default constructor. `arrayList1` is initialized for a specific initial capacity. `arrayList2` is initialized using an element of another collection.

The `ArrayList` properties and methods are important to add, store, or remove our data items from our collections. There are many properties and methods available for the `ArrayList` class. In the upcoming sections, we will discuss commonly used methods and properties.

Properties

The properties of `ArrayList` play a vital role while analysing an existing `ArrayList`; the following are the commonly used properties:

Property	Description
Capacity	A getter setter property; with the use of this, we can set or get the number of elements of `ArrayList`. For example: `ArrayList arrayList = new ArrayList {Capacity = 50};`

Count	Total actual number of elements `ArrayList` contains. Please note that this count may differ from capacity.
	For example:
	`ArrayList arrayList = new ArrayList {Capacity = 50};`
	`var numRandom = new Random(50);`
	`for (var countIndex = 0; countIndex < 50; countIndex++)`
	`arrayList.Add(numRandom.Next(50));`

IsFixedSize	A getter property returns true/false on the basis of whether `ArrayList` is of fixed size or not.
	For example:
	`ArrayList arrayList = new ArrayList();`
	`var arrayListIsFixedSize = arrayList.IsFixedSize;`

Methods

As we discussed in the previous section, properties play important roles while we're working with `ArrayList`. In the same node, methods provide us a way to add, remove, or perform other operations while working with non-generic collections:

Method	Description

`Add (object value)`	Adds an object to the end of `ArrayList`.
	For example:
	`ArrayList arrayList = new ArrayList {Capacity = 50};`
	`var numRandom = new Random(50);`
	`for (var countIndex = 0; countIndex < 50;`
	`countIndex++)`
	`arrayList.Add(numRandom.Next(50));`

`Void Clear()`	Removes all elements from `ArrayList`. For example: `arrayList.Clear();`
`Void Remove(object obj)`	Removes first occurred element in the collection. For example: `arrayList.Remove(15);`
`Void Sort()`	Sorts all the elements in `ArrayList`

The following code snippet is a complete example showing `ArrayList`:

```
public void ArrayListExample(int count)
{
var arrayList = new ArrayList();
var numRandom = new Random(count);
WriteLine($"Creating an ArrayList with capacity: {count}");
for (var countIndex = 0; countIndex < count; countIndex++)
arrayList.Add(numRandom.Next(count));
WriteLine($"Capacity: {arrayList.Capacity}");
WriteLine($"Count: {arrayList.Count}");
Write("ArrayList original contents: ");
PrintArrayListContents(arrayList);
WriteLine();
arrayList.Reverse();
Write("ArrayList reversed contents: ");
PrintArrayListContents(arrayList);
WriteLine();
Write("ArrayList sorted Content: ");
arrayList.Sort();
PrintArrayListContents(arrayList);
```

```
WriteLine();
ReadKey();
}
```

The following is the output of the preceding program:

```
Enter arrayList size: 15
Creating an ArrayList with capacity: 15
Capacity: 16
Count: 15
ArrayList original contents: 8 3 3 11 14 10 9 14 12 12 5 2 14 4 7
ArrayList reversed contents: 7 4 14 2 5 12 12 14 9 10 14 11 3 3 8
ArrayList sorted Content: 2 3 3 4 5 7 8 9 10 11 12 12 14 14 14
```

You will learn all advanced concepts of collections and generics on day six.

HashTable

A non-generic type, the hashTable class is nothing but a representation of collections of key/value pairs and is organized on the basis of a key, which is nothing but a hash code. The use of hashTable is advisable when we need to access data on the basis of a key.

Declaration of HashTable

Hashtable can be declared by initializing the Hashtable class; the following code snippet shows the same:

```
Hashtable hashtable = new Hashtable();
```

We will discuss commonly used methods and properties of HashTable next.

Properties

The properties of `hashTable` play a vital role while analyzing an existing `HashTable`; the following are the commonly used properties:

Property	Description

Count	A getter property; returns number of key/value pairs in the `HashTable`. For example:
	
	```var hashtable = new Hashtable```
	```{```
	```{1, "Gaurav Aroraa"},```
	```{2, "Vikas Tiwari"},```
	```{3, "Denim Pinto"},```
	```{4, "Diwakar"},```
	```{5, "Merint"}```
	```};```
	```var count = hashtable.Count;```

IsFixedSize	A getter property; returns true/false on the basis of whether the `HashTable` is of fixed size or not. For example:
	
	```var hashtable = new Hashtable```
	```{```
	```{1, "Gaurav Aroraa"},```
	```{2, "Vikas Tiwari"},```
	```{3, "Denim Pinto"},```
	```{4, "Diwakar"},```
	```{5, "Merint"}```
	```};```
	```var fixedSize = hashtable.IsFixedSize ? " fixed size." : " not```
	```fixed size.";```
	```WriteLine($"HashTable is {fixedSize} .");```

IsReadOnly	A getter property; tells us whether `Hashtable` is read-only or not. For example: ```WriteLine($"HashTable is ReadOnly : {hashtable.IsReadOnly} ");```

Methods

The methods of `HashTable` provide a way to add, remove, and analyze the collection by providing more operations, as discussed in the following table:

Method	Description

`Add (object key, object value)`	Adds an element of a specific key and value to `HashTable`. For example:
	```var hashtable = new Hashtable```
	```hashtable.Add(11,"Rama");```

`Void Clear()`	Removes all elements from `HashTable`. For example: ```hashtable.Clear();```
`Void Remove (object key)`	Removes element of a specified key from HashTable. For example: ```hashtable.Remove(15);```

In the following section, we will implement a simple `HashTable` with the use of a code snippet where we will create a `HashTable` collection, and will try to reiterate its keys:

```
public void HashTableExample()
{
    WriteLine("Creating HashTable");
    var hashtable = new Hashtable
    {
        {1, "Gaurav Aroraa"},
        {2, "Vikas Tiwari"},
        {3, "Denim Pinto"},
        {4, "Diwakar"},
        {5, "Merint"}
    };
    WriteLine("Reading HashTable Keys");
    foreach (var hashtableKey in hashtable.Keys)
    {
        WriteLine($"Key :{hashtableKey} - value :
        {hashtable[hashtableKey]}");
    }
}
```

The following is the output of the preceding code:

```
Creating HashTable
Reading HashTable Keys
Key :5 - value : Merint
Key :4 - value : Diwakar
Key :3 - value : Denim Pinto
Key :2 - value : Vikas Tiwari
Key :1 - value : Gaurav Aroraa
Press any key...
```

SortedList

A non-generic type, the SortedList class is nothing but a representation of collections of key/value pairs, organized on the basis of a key, and is sorted by key. SortedList is a combination of ArrayList and HashTable. So, we can access the elements by key or index.

Declaration of SortedList

SortedList can be declared by initializing the SortedList class; the following code snippet shows the same:

```
SortedList sortedList = new SortedList();
```

We will discuss commonly used methods and properties of SortedList next.

Properties

The properties of SortedList play a vital role while analyzing an existing SortedList; the following are the commonly used properties:

Property	Description

Capacity	A getter setter property; with the use of this, we can set or get the capacity of SortedList.
	For example:
	<pre>var sortedList = new SortedList
	{
	{1, "Gaurav Aroraa"},
	{2, "Vikas Tiwari"},
	{3, "Denim Pinto"},
	{4, "Diwakar"},
	{5, "Merint"},
	{11, "Rama"}
	};
	WriteLine($"Capacity: {sortedList.Capacity}");</pre>

Count	A getter property; returns number of key/value pairs in the HashTable.
	For example:
	<pre>var sortedList = new SortedList
	{
	{1, "Gaurav Aroraa"},
	{2, "Vikas Tiwari"},
	{3, "Denim Pinto"},
	{4, "Diwakar"},
	{5, "Merint"},
	{11, "Rama"}
	};
	WriteLine($"Capacity: {sortedList.Count}");</pre>

`IsFixedSize`	A getter property; returns true/false on the basis of whether `SortedList` is of fixed size or not.
	For example:
	<pre>var sortedList = new SortedList
	{
	{1, "Gaurav Aroraa"},
	{2, "Vikas Tiwari"},
	{3, "Denim Pinto"},
	{4, "Diwakar"},
	{5, "Merint"},
	{11, "Rama"}
	};
	ar fixedSize = sortedList.IsFixedSize ? " fixed size." : " not
	fixed size.";
	WriteLine($"SortedList is {fixedSize} .");</pre>

`IsReadOnly`	A getter property; tells us whether `SortedList` is read-only or not. For example: <pre>WriteLine($"SortedList is ReadOnly : {sortedList.IsReadOnly} ");</pre>

Methods

The following are the commonly used methods:

Method	Description

`Add (object key, object value)`	Adds an element of a specific key and value to `SortedList`.
	For example:
	<pre>var sortedList = new SortedList
	sortedList.Add(11, "Rama");</pre>

`Void Clear()`	Removes all elements from `SortedList`. For example: <pre>sortedList.Clear();</pre>
`Void Remove (object key)`	Removes an element of specified key from `SortedList`. For example: <pre>sortedList.Remove(15);</pre>

In the upcoming section, we will implement code with the use of the properties and methods mentioned in previous sections. Let's collect a list of all stakeholders of the book *Learn C# in 7 days* with the use of `SortedList`:

```
public void SortedListExample()
{
    WriteLine("Creating SortedList");
```

```
var sortedList = new SortedList
{
    {1, "Gaurav Aroraa"},
    {2, "Vikas Tiwari"},
    {3, "Denim Pinto"},
    {4, "Diwakar"},
    {5, "Merint"},
    {11, "Rama"}
};
WriteLine("Reading SortedList Keys");
WriteLine($"Capacity: {sortedList.Capacity}");
WriteLine($"Count: {sortedList.Count}");
var fixedSize = sortedList.IsFixedSize ? " fixed
size." :" not fixed size.";
WriteLine($"SortedList is {fixedSize} .");
WriteLine($"SortedList is ReadOnly :
{sortedList.IsReadOnly} ");
foreach (var key in sortedList.Keys)
{
    WriteLine($"Key :{key} - value :
    {sortedList[key]}");
}
}
```

The following is the output of the preceding code:

```
Creating SortedList
Reading SortedList Keys
Capacity: 16
Count: 6
SortedList is  not fixed size. .
SortedList is ReadOnly : False
Key :1 - value : Gaurav Aroraa
Key :2 - value : Vikas Tiwari
Key :3 - value : Denim Pinto
Key :4 - value : Diwakar
Key :5 - value : Merint
Key :11 - value : Rama
Press any key...
```

Stack

A non-generic type, it represents a collection as **last in, first out (LIFO)** of objects. It contains two main things: `Push` and `Pop`. Whenever we're inserting an item into the list, it is called pushing, and when we extract/remove an item from the list, it's called popping. When we get an object without removing the item from the list, it is called peeking.

Declaration of Stack

The declaration of `Stack` is very similar to the way we declared other non-generic types. The following code snippet shows the same:

```
Stack stackList = new Stack();
```

We will discuss commonly used methods and properties of `Stack`.

Properties

The `Stack` class has only one property, which tells the count:

Property	Description

Count	A getter property; returns number of elements a stack contains. For example:
	`var stackList = new Stack();`
	`stackList.Push("Gaurav Aroraa");`
	`stackList.Push("Vikas Tiwari");`
	`stackList.Push("Denim Pinto");`
	`stackList.Push("Diwakar");`
	`stackList.Push("Merint");`
	`WriteLine($"Count: {stackList.Count}");`

Methods

The following are the commonly used methods:

Method	Description

Object Peek()	Returns the object at the top of the stack but does not remove it.
	For example:
	`WriteLine($"Next value without`
	`removing:{stackList.Peek()}");`

Object Pop()	Removes and returns the object at the top of the stack. For example: `WriteLine($"Remove item: {stackList.Pop()}");`

Void Push(object obj)	Inserts an object at the top of the stack. For example:
	`WriteLine("Adding more items.");`
	`stackList.Push("Rama");`
	`stackList.Push("Shama");`

Void Clear()	Removes all elements from the stack. For example:
	`var stackList = new Stack();`
	`stackList.Push("Gaurav Aroraa");`
	`stackList.Push("Vikas Tiwari");`
	`stackList.Push("Denim Pinto");`
	`stackList.Push("Diwakar");`
	`stackList.Push("Merint");`
	`stackList.Clear();`

The following is the complete example of stack:

```
public void StackExample()
{
    WriteLine("Creating Stack");
    var stackList = new Stack();
    stackList.Push("Gaurav Aroraa");
    stackList.Push("Vikas Tiwari");
    stackList.Push("Denim Pinto");
    stackList.Push("Diwakar");
    stackList.Push("Merint");
    WriteLine("Reading stack items");
    ReadingStack(stackList);
    WriteLine();
    WriteLine($"Count: {stackList.Count}");
    WriteLine("Adding more items.");
    stackList.Push("Rama");
    stackList.Push("Shama");
    WriteLine();
    WriteLine($"Count: {stackList.Count}");
    WriteLine($"Next value without removing:
    {stackList.Peek()}");
    WriteLine();
    WriteLine("Reading stack items.");
    ReadingStack(stackList);
    WriteLine();
    WriteLine("Remove value");
```

```
        stackList.Pop();
        WriteLine();
        WriteLine("Reading stack items after removing an
        item.");
        ReadingStack(stackList);
        ReadLine();
    }
```

The previous code captures a list of stakeholders for the book *Learning C# in 7 days* using `Stack`, and showing the usage of properties and methods discussed in previous sections. This code resulted in the output shown in the following screenshot:

```
Diwakar
Denim Pinto
Vikas Tiwari
Gaurav Aroraa

Count: 5
Adding more items.

Count: 7
Next value without removing:Shama

Reading stack items.
Shama
Rama
Merint
Diwakar
Denim Pinto
Vikas Tiwari
Gaurav Aroraa

Remove value

Reading stack items after removing an item.
Rama
Merint
Diwakar
Denim Pinto
Vikas Tiwari
Gaurav Aroraa
```

Queue

Queue is just a non-generic type that represents a FIFO collection of an object. There are two main actions of `queue`: when adding an item, it is called enqueuer, and when removing an item, it is called `dequeue`.

Declaration of Queue

The declaration of `Queue` is very similar to the way we declared other non-generic types. The following code snippet shows the same:

```
Queue queue = new Queue();
```

We will discuss commonly used methods and properties of `Queue` next.

Properties

The `Queue` class has only one property, which tells the count:

Property	Description
Count	A getter property; returns the number of elements `queue` contained. For example: `Queue queue = new Queue();` `queue.Enqueue("Gaurav Aroraa");` `queue.Enqueue("Vikas Tiwari");` `queue.Enqueue("Denim Pinto");` `queue.Enqueue("Diwakar");` `queue.Enqueue("Merint");` `WriteLine($"Count: {queue.Count}");`

Methods

The following are the commonly used methods:

Method	Description
Object Peek()	Returns the object at the top of the `queue` but does not remove it. For example: `WriteLine($"Next value without removing:{stackList.Peek()}");`

`Object Dequeue()`	Removes and returns the object at the beginning of the `queue`. For example: `WriteLine($"Remove item: {queue.Dequeue()}");`
`Void Enqueue (object obj)`	Inserts an object at the end of the `queue`. For example: `WriteLine("Adding more items.");` `queue.Enqueue("Rama");`
`Void Clear()`	Removes all elements from `Queue`. For example: `Queue queue = new Queue();` `queue.Enqueue("Gaurav Aroraa");` `queue.Enqueue("Vikas Tiwari");` `queue.Enqueue("Denim Pinto");` `queue.Enqueue("Diwakar");` `queue.Enqueue("Merint");` `queue.Clear();`

The previous sections discussed properties and methods. Now it's time to implement these properties and methods in a real-world implementation. Let's create a `queue` that contains stockholders names for the book *Learn C# in 7 days*. The following code snippet is using the `Enqueue` and `Dequeue` methods to add and remove the items from the collections stored using `queue`:

```
public void QueueExample()
{
    WriteLine("Creating Queue");
    var queue = new Queue();
    queue.Enqueue("Gaurav Aroraa");
    queue.Enqueue("Vikas Tiwari");
    queue.Enqueue("Denim Pinto");
    queue.Enqueue("Diwakar");
    queue.Enqueue("Merint");
    WriteLine("Reading Queue items");
    ReadingQueue(queue);
    WriteLine();
    WriteLine($"Count: {queue.Count}");
    WriteLine("Adding more items.");
    queue.Enqueue("Rama");
    queue.Enqueue("Shama");
    WriteLine();
    WriteLine($"Count: {queue.Count}");
    WriteLine($"Next value without removing:
    {queue.Peek()}");
    WriteLine();
```

```
        WriteLine("Reading queue items.");
        ReadingQueue(queue);
        WriteLine();
        WriteLine($"Remove item: {queue.Dequeue()}");
        WriteLine();
        WriteLine("Reading queue items after removing an
        item.");
        ReadingQueue(queue);
}
```

The following is the output of the preceding code:

```
Creating Queue
Reading Queue items
Gaurav Aroraa
Vikas Tiwari
Denim Pinto
Diwakar
Merint

Count: 5
Adding more items.

Count: 7
Next value without removing:Gaurav Aroraa

Reading queue items.
Gaurav Aroraa
Vikas Tiwari
Denim Pinto
Diwakar
Merint
Rama
Shama

Remove item: Gaurav Aroraa

Reading queue items after removing an item.
Vikas Tiwari
Denim Pinto
Diwakar
Merint
Rama
Shama
Press any key...
```

BitArray

BitArray is nothing but an array which manages an array of bit values. These values are represented as Boolean. True means bit is *ON* (1) and false means bit is *OFF*(0). This non-generic collection class is important when we need to store the bits.

The implementation of BitArray is not covered. Please refer to the exercises at the end of the chapter to implement BitArray.

 We have discussed non-generic collections in this chapter. Generic collections are beyond the scope of this chapter; we will cover them on day six. To compare different collections, refer to `https://www.codeproject.com/Articles/832189/List-vs-IEnumerable-vs-IQueryable-vs-ICollection-v`.

Hands - on exercise

Solve the following questions, which cover the concepts from today's learning:

1. What is reflection? Write a short program to use `System.Type`.
2. Create a class that contains at least three properties, two constructors, two public methods, and three private methods, and implements at least one interface.
3. Write a program with the use of `System.Reflection.Extensins` to assess the class created in question two.
4. Study the NuGet package `System.Reflection.TypeExtensions` and write a program by implementing all of its features.
5. Study the NuGet package `System.Reflection. Primitives` and write a program by implementing all of its features.
6. What are delegate types and how can you define multicast delegates?
7. What are events? How are events are based on the publisher-subscriber model? Show this with the use of a real-world example.
8. Write a program using delegates and events to get an output similar to `https://github.com/garora/TDD-Katas#string-sum-kata`.
9. Define collections and implement non-generic types.

 Refer to our problem from day one, the vowel count problem, and implement this using all non-generic collection types.

Revisiting Day 05

Today, we have discussed very important concepts of C#, covering reflection, collections, delegates, and events.

We discussed the importance of reflection in our code analysis approach. During the discussion, we implemented code showing the power of reflection, where we analyzed the complete code.

Then we discussed delegates and events and how delegates and events work in C#. We also implemented delegates and events.

One of the important and key features of the C# language that we discussed in detail was non-generic types, namely `ArrayList`, `HashTable`, `SortedList`, `Queue`, `Stack`, and so on. We implemented all these using C# 7.0 code.

6

Day 06 - Deep Dive with Advanced Concepts

Today is day six of our seven-day learning series. On day five, we discussed important concepts of the C# language and went through reflection, collections, delegates, and events. We explored these concepts using a code snippet, where we discussed non-generic collections. Today, we will discuss the main power of collections using generic types, and then, we will cover preprocessor directives and attributes.

We will cover the following topics in this chapter:

- Playing with collections and generics
- Beautifying code using attributes
- Leveraging Preprocessor Directives
- Getting started with LINQ
- Writing unsafe code
- Writing asynchronous code
- Revisiting Day 6
- Hands-on exercise

Playing with collections and generics

Collections are not new for us, as we went through and discussed non-generic collections on day five. So, we also have generic collections. In this section, we will discuss all about collections and generics with the use of code examples.

Understanding collection classes and their usage

As discussed on day five, collection classes are specialized classes and are meant for data interaction (storage and retrieval). We have already discussed various collection classes, namely
stacks, queues, lists, and hash tables, and we have written code using the `System.Collections.NonGeneric` namespace. The following table provides us an overview of the usage and meaning of non-generic collection classes:

Property	Description	Usage
ArrayList	The name itself describes that this contains a collection of ordered collection that can be accessed using index. We can declare `ArrayList` as follows: `ArrayList arrayList = new ArrayList();`	On day two, we discussed arrays and went through how to access the individual elements of an array. In the case of `ArrayList`, we can get the benefits of various methods to add or remove elements of collections, as discussed on day five.
HashTable	`HashTable` is nothing but a representation of collections of a key-value-pair and are organized on the basis of a key, which is nothing more than a hash code. The use of `HashTable` is advisable when we need to access data on the basis of a key. We can declare `HashTable` as follows: `Hashtable hashtable = new Hashtable();`	`HashTable` is very useful when we need to access elements with the use of a key. In such scenarios, we have a key and need to find values in the collection on the basis of a key.

SortedList	The `SortedList` class is nothing but a representation of collections of a key-value-pair and are organized on the basis of a key and are sorted by key. `SortedList` classes are a combination of `ArrayList` and `HashTable`. So, we can access the elements using the key or the index. We can declare `SortedList` as follows: `SortedList sortedList = new SortedList();`	As stated, a sorted list is a combination of an array and a hash table. Items can be accessed using a key or an index. This is `ArrayList` when items are accessed using an index; on the other hand, it is `HashTable` when items are accessed using a hash key. The main thing in `SortedList` is that the collection of items is always sorted by the key value.
Stack	Stack represents a collection of objects; the objects are accessible in the order of **Last In First Out (LIFO)**. It contains two main operations: push and pop. Whenever we insert an item to the list, it is called pushing, and when we extract/remove an item from the list, it is called popping. When we get an object without removing the item from the list, it is called peeking. We can declare it as follows: `Stack stackList = new Stack();`	This is important to use when items that were inserted last need to be retrieved first.
Queue	Queue represents a **First In First Out(FIFO)** collection of objects. There are two main actions in queue-- adding an item is called enqueue and removing an item is called deque. We can declare a Queue as follows: `Queue queue = new Queue();`	This is important when items that were inserted first need to be retrieved first.
BitArray	`BitArray` is nothing but an array that manages an array of bit values. These values are represented as Boolean. True means *ON* (1) and False means *OFF*(0). We can declare `BitArray` as follows: `BitArray bitArray = new BitArray(8);`	This non-generic collection class is important when we need to store the bits.

The preceding table only shows non-generic collection classes. With the use of generics, we can also implement generic collection classes by taking the help of the `System.Collections` namespace. In the coming sections, we will discuss generic collection classes.

Performance - BitArray versus boolArray

In the previous table, we discussed that `BitArray` is just an array that manages true or false values (*0* or *1*). But internally, `BitArray` performed round eight per element for a Byte and undergoes in various logical operations and need more CPU cycles. On the other hand, a `boolArray` (`bool[]`) stores each element as 1-byte, so it takes more memory but requires fewer CPU cycles. `BitArray` over `bool[]` is memory optimizer.

Let's consider the following performance test and see how `BitArray` performs:

```
private static long BitArrayTest(int max)
{
    Stopwatch stopwatch = Stopwatch.StartNew();
    var bitarray = new BitArray(max);
    for (int index = 0; index < bitarray.Length; index++)
    {
        bitarray[index] = !bitarray[index];
        WriteLine($"'bitarray[{index}]' = {bitarray[index]}");
    }
    stopwatch.Stop();
    return stopwatch.ElapsedMilliseconds;
}
```

In the preceding code snippet, we are just testing `BitArray` performance by applying a very simple test, where we run a for loop up to the maximum count of int `MaxValue`.

The following code snippet is for a simple test performed for `bool[]` to make this test simpler; we just initiated a for loop up to the maximum value of `int.MaxValue`:

```
private static long BoolArrayTest(int max)
{
    Stopwatch stopwatch = Stopwatch.StartNew();
    var boolArray = new bool[max];
    for (int index = 0; index < boolArray.Length; index++)
    {
        boolArray[index] = !boolArray[index];
        WriteLine($"'boolArray[{index}]' = {boolArray[index]}");
    }
    stopwatch.Stop();
```

```
        return stopwatch.ElapsedMilliseconds;
    }
```

The following code snippet makes a call to the `BitArrayTest` and `BoolArrayTest` methods:

```
private static void BitArrayBoolArrayPerformance()
{
    //This is a simple test
    //Not testing bitwiseshift  etc.
    WriteLine("BitArray vs. Bool Array performance test.\n");
    WriteLine($"Total elements of bit array: {int.MaxValue}");
    PressAnyKey();
    WriteLine("Starting BitArray Test:");
    var bitArrayTestResult = BitArrayTest(int.MaxValue);
    WriteLine("Ending BitArray Test:");
    WriteLine($"Total timeElapsed: {bitArrayTestResult}");

    WriteLine("\nStarting BoolArray Test:");
    WriteLine($"Total elements of bit array: {int.MaxValue}");
    PressAnyKey();
    var boolArrayTestResult = BoolArrayTest(int.MaxValue);
    WriteLine("Ending BitArray Test:");
    WriteLine($"Total timeElapsed: {boolArrayTestResult}");
}
```

On my machine, `BitArrayTest` took six seconds and `BoolArrayTest` took 15 seconds.

From the preceding tests we can conclude that bool arrays consume eight times the size/space that could represent the values. In simpler words, bool arrays require 1 byte per element.

Understanding generics and their usage

In simple words, with the help of generics, we can create or write code for a class that is meant to accept different data types for which it is written. Let's say if a generic class is written in a way to accept a structure, then it will accept int, string, or custom structures. This class is also known as a generic class. This works more magically when it allows us to define the data type when we declare an instance of this generic class. Let's study the following code snippet, where we define a generic class and provide data types on the creation of its instance:

```
IList<Person> persons = new List<Person>()
```

In the previous code snippet, we declare a `persons` variable of a generic type, `List`. Here, we have `Person` as a strong type. The following is the complete code snippet that populates this strongly typed list:

```
private static IEnumerable<Person> CreatePersonList()
    {
        IList<Person> persons = new List<Person>
        {
            new Person
            {
                FirstName = "Denim",
                LastName = "Pinto",
                Age = 31
            },
            new Person
            {
                FirstName = "Vikas",
                LastName = "Tiwari",
                Age = 25
            },
            new Person
            {
                FirstName = "Shivprasad",
                LastName = "Koirala",
                Age = 40
            },
            new Person
            {
                FirstName = "Gaurav",
                LastName = "Aroraa",
                Age = 43
            }
        };

        return persons;
    }
```

The preceding code snippet showed the initiation of a list of the `Person` type and its collection items. These items can be iterated as mentioned in the following code snippet:

```
private static void Main(string[] args)
    {
        WriteLine("Person list:");
        foreach (var person in Person.GetPersonList())
        {
            WriteLine($"Name:{person.FirstName} {person.LastName}");
            WriteLine($"Age:{person.Age}");
        }
```

```
        ReadLine();
    }
```

We will get the following output after running the preceding code snippet:

```
Person list:
Name:Denim Pinto
Age:31
Name:Vikas Tiwari
Age:25
Name:Shivprasad Koirala
Age:40
Name:Gaurav Aroraa
Age:43
```

We can create a generic list to a strongly typed list, which can accept types other than
`Person`. For this, we just need to create a list like this:

```
private IEnumerable<T> CreateGenericList<T>()
{
    IList<T> persons = new List<T>();
    //other stuffs

    return persons;
}
```

In the preceding code snippet `T` could be `Person` or any related type.

Collections and generics

On day two, you learned about arrays of a fixed size. You can use fixed-size arrays for
strongly typed list objects. But what if we want to use or organize these objects into other
data structures, such as queue, list, stack, and so on? We can achieve all these with the use
of collections (`System.Collections`).

`System.Collections` (`https://www.nuget.org/packages/System.Collections/`) is a NuGet package that provides all the generic types, and the following are the frequently used types:

Generic collection types	Description
`System.Collections.Generic.List<T>`	A strongly typed generic list
`System.Collections.Generic.Dictionary<TKey, TValue>`	A strongly typed generic dictionary with a key-value pair
`System.Collections.Generic.Queue<T>`	A generic `Queue`
`System.Collections.Generic.Stack<T>`	A generic `Stack`
`System.Collections.Generic.HashSet<T>`	A generic `HashSet`
`System.Collections.Generic.LinkedList<T>`	A generic `LinkedList`
`System.Collections.Generic.SortedDictionary<TKey, TValue>`	A generic `SortedDictionary` with a key-value pair collection and sorted on key.

The preceding table is just an overview of generic classes of the `System.Collections.Generics` namespace. In the coming sections, we will discuss generic collections in detail with the help of code examples.

For a complete list of classes, structures, and interfaces of the `System.Collections.Generics` namespace, visit the official documentations link at `https://docs.microsoft.com/en-us/dotnet/api/system.collections.generic?view=netcore-2.0`.

Why should we use generics?

For non-generic lists, we use collections from the universal base of the object type [https://docs.microsoft.com/en-us/dotnet/api/system.object], which is not type-safe at compile time. Let's assume that we are using a non-generic collection of ArrayList; see the following code snippet for more details:

```
ArrayList authorArrayList = new ArrayList {"Gaurav Aroraa", "43"};
foreach (string author in authorArrayList)
{
    WriteLine($"Name:{author}");
}
```

Here, we have an ArrayList with string values. Here, we have the age as a string which actually should be int. Let's take another ArrayList, which has the age as an int:

```
ArrayList editorArrayList = new ArrayList { "Vikas Tiwari", 25 };
foreach (int editor in editorArrayList)
{
    WriteLine($"Name:{editor}");
}
```

In this case, our code compiles, but it will throw an exception of typecast at runtime. So, our ArrayList does not have compile-time type checking:

After digging through the preceding code, we can easily understand why there is no error at compile time; this is because, `ArrayList` accepts any type (both value and reference) and then casts it to a universal base type of .NET, which is nothing but object. But when we run the code at that time, it requires the actual type, for example, if it is defined as string, then it should be of the string type at runtime and not of the object type. Hence, we get a runtime exception.

 The activity of casting, boxing, and unboxing of an object in `ArrayList` hits the performance, and it depends upon the size of `ArrayList` and how large the data that you're iterating through is.

With the help of the preceding code example, we came to know two drawbacks of a non-generic `ArrayList`:

1. It is not compile-time type-safe.
2. Impacts the performance while dealing with large data.
3. `ArrayList` casts everything to object, so there is no way to stop adding any type of items at compile time. For example, in the preceding code snippet, we can enter int and/or string type items.

To overcome such issues/drawbacks, we have generic collections, which prevent us from supplying anything other than the expected type. Consider the following code snippet:

```
List<string> authorName = new List<string> {"Gaurav Aroraa"};
```

We have a `List`, which is defined to get only string type items. So, we can add only string type values here. Now consider the following:

```
List<string> authorName = new List<string>();
authorName.Add("Gaurav Aroraa");
authorName.Add(43);
```

Here, we're trying to supply an item of the int type (remember that we did the same thing in the case of `ArrayList`). Now, we get a compile-time error that is related to casting, so a generic list that is defined to accept only string type items has the capability to stop the client from entering items of any type other than string. If we hover the mouse on the `43`, it shows the complete error; refer to the following image:

```
0 references | Gaursv Arora, 1 day ago | 1 author, 2 changes
private static void Main(string[] args)
{

    List<string> authorName = new List<string>();
    authorName.Add("Gaurav Aroraa");
    authorName.Add(43);

}                          Argument 1: cannot convert from 'int' to 'string'

                           Argument type 'int' is not assignable to parameter type 'string'
```

In the preceding code snippet, we resolved our one problem by declaring a list of string, which only allows us to enter string values, so in the case of authors, we can only enter author names but not author age. You may be thinking that if we need another list of type int that provides us a way to enter the author's age, that is, if we need a separate list for a new type, then why should we use generic collections? At the moment, we need only two items--name and age--so we are creating two different lists of the string and int type on this node. If we need another item of a different type, then will we be going for another new list. This is the time when we have things of multiple types, such as string, int, decimal, and so on. We can create our own types. Consider the following declaration of a generic list:

```
List<Person> persons = new List<Person>();
```

We have a `List` of type `Person`. This generic list will allow all types of items that are defined in this type. The following is our `Person` class:

```
internal class Person
{
    public string FirstName { get; set; }
    public string LastName { get; set; }
    public int Age { get; set; }
}
```

Our `Person` class contains three properties, two of type string and one is of type int. Here, we have a complete solution for the problems we discussed in the previous section. With the help of this List, which is of the `Person` type, we can enter an item of the string and/or int type. The following code snippet shows this in action:

```
private static void PersonList()
{
    List<Person> persons = new List<Person>
    {
        new Person
        {
```

```
                FirstName = "Gaurav",
                LastName = "Aroraa",
                Age = 43
            }
    };
    WriteLine("Person list:");
    foreach (var person in persons)
    {
        WriteLine($"Name:{person.FirstName} {person.LastName}");
        WriteLine($"Age:{person.Age}");
    }
}
```

After running this code, the following will be our output:

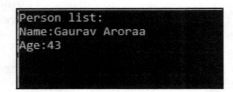

Our `List` of the `Person` type will be more performant than `ArrayList`, as in our generic class, there is not implicit typecast to object; the items are rather of their expected types.

Discussing constraints

In the previous section, we discussed how a `List` of the `Person` type accepts all the items of their defined types. In our example code, we only use the string and int data types, but in generics, you can use any data type, including int, float, double, and so on. On the other hand, there may be scenarios where we want to restrict our use to a few data types or only a specific data type in generics. To achieve this, there are generic constraints. Consider the following code snippet:

```
public class GenericConstraint<T> where T:class
{
    public T ImplementIt(T value)
    {
        return value;
    }
}
```

Here, our class is a generic class. GenericConstraint, of type `T`, which is nothing but a reference type; hence, we created this class to accept only the reference type. No value type will be accepted by this class. This class has an `ImplementIt` method, which accepts a parameter of type `T` and returns a value of type `T`.

 Check `https://docs.microsoft.com/en-us/dotnet/csharp/programming-guide/generics/generic-type-parameters` to know more about Generic Type Parameter Guidelines.

The following declarations are valid as these are of the reference types:

```
GenericConstraint<string> genericConstraint = new
GenericConstraint<string>();
Person person = genericPersonConstraint.ImplementIt(new Person());
```

The following is an invalid declaration, as this is of the value type, which is not meant for the current generic class:

```
GenericConstraint<int> genericConstraint = new GenericConstraint<int>();
```

On day two, we learned that int is a value type and not a reference type. The preceding declaration gives a compile-time error. In Visual Studio, you will see the following error:

```
0 references | Gaurav Arora, 1 day ago | 1 author, 2 changes
private static void Main(string[] args)
{
    GenericConstraint<int> genericConstraint = new GenericConstraint<int>();
}
```

The type 'int' must be a reference type in order to use it as parameter 'T' in the generic type or method 'GenericConstraint<T>'

The type 'int' must be a reference type in order to use it as parameter 'T'

So, with the help of generic constraints, we restrict our class to not accept any types other than reference types.

 Constraints are basically an act by which you safeguard your generic class to prevent the client from using any other type while the class is instantiated. It results in a compile-time error if the client code tries to provide a type that is not allowed. The contextual where keyword helps us in defining constraints.

In the real world, you can define various type of constraints and these would restrict client code to create any unwanted situation. Let's discuss these types with examples:

The value type

This constraint is defined with the contextual keyword, `where T: struct`. With this constraint, the client's code should contain an argument of the value type; here, any value except Nullable can be specified.

Example

The following is a code snippet declaring a generic class with a value type constraint:

```
public class ValueTypeConstraint<T> where T : struct
{
    public T ImplementIt(T value)
    {
        return value;
    }
}
```

Usage

The following is a code snippet that describes the client code of a generic class declared with a value type constraint:

```
private static void ImplementValueTypeGenericClass()
{
    const int age = 43;
    ValueTypeConstraint<int> valueTypeConstraint = new
    ValueTypeConstraint<int>();
    WriteLine($"Age:{valueTypeConstraint.ImplementIt(age)}");

}
```

The reference type

This constraint is defined with the contextual keyword, `where T:class`. Using this constraint, the client code is bound to not provide any types other than reference types. Valid types are class, interface, delegate, and array.

Example

The following code snippet declares a generic class with a reference type constraint:

```
public class ReferenceTypeConstraint<T> where T:class
{
    public T ImplementIt(T value)
    {
        return value;
    }
}
```

Usage

The following code snippet describes the client code of a generic class declared with a reference type constraint:

```
private static void ImplementReferenceTypeGenericClass()
{
    const string thisIsAuthorName = "Gaurav Aroraa";
    ReferenceTypeConstraint<string> referenceTypeConstraint = new
ReferenceTypeConstraint<string>();
WriteLine($"Name:{referenceTypeConstraint.ImplementIt(thisIsAuthorName)}");

    ReferenceTypeConstraint<Person> referenceTypePersonConstraint = new
ReferenceTypeConstraint<Person>();

    Person person = referenceTypePersonConstraint.ImplementIt(new Person
    {
        FirstName = "Gaurav",
        LastName = "Aroraa",
        Age = 43
    });
    WriteLine($"Name:{person.FirstName}{person.LastName}");
    WriteLine($"Age:{person.Age}");
}
```

The default constructor

This constraint is defined with the contextual keyword, `where T: new()`, and it restricts generic type parameters from defining default constructors. It is also compulsory that an argument of type `T` must have a public parameterless constructor. The `new()` constraint must be specified in the end, when used with other constraints.

Example

The following code snippet declares a generic class with a default constructor constraint:

```
public class DefaultConstructorConstraint<T> where T : new()
{
    public T ImplementIt(T value)
    {
        return value;
    }
}
```

Usage

The following code snippet describes the client code of a generic class declared with a default constructor constraint:

```
private static void ImplementDefaultConstructorGenericClass()
{
    DefaultConstructorConstraint<ClassWithDefautConstructor>
    constructorConstraint = new
    DefaultConstructorConstraint<ClassWithDefautConstructor>();
    var result = constructorConstraint.ImplementIt(new
    ClassWithDefautConstructor { Name = "Gaurav Aroraa" });
    WriteLine($"Name:{result.Name}");
}
```

The base class constraint

This constraint is defined with the contextual keyword, `where T: <BaseClass>`. This constraint restricts all the client code where the supplied arguments are not of, or not derived from, the specified base class.

Example

The following code snippet declares a generic class with the base class constraint:

```
public class BaseClassConstraint<T> where T:Person
{
    public T ImplementIt(T value)
    {
        return value;
    }
}
```

Usage

The following is a code snippet describes the client code of a generic class declared with a base class constraint:

```
private static void ImplementBaseClassConstraint()
{
    BaseClassConstraint<Author>baseClassConstraint = new
BaseClassConstraint<Author>();
    var result = baseClassConstraint.ImplementIt(new Author
    {
        FirstName = "Shivprasad",
        LastName = "Koirala",
         Age = 40
    });

    WriteLine($"Name:{result.FirstName} {result.LastName}");
    WriteLine($"Age:{result.Age}");
}
```

The interface constraint

This constraint is defined with the contextual keyword, `where T:<interface name>`. The client code must supply a parameter of the type that implements the specified parameter. There may be multiple interfaces defined in this constraint.

Example

The following code snippet declares a generic class with an interface constraint:

```
public class InterfaceConstraint<T>:IDisposable where T : IDisposable
{
    public T ImplementIt(T value)
    {
        return value;
    }

    public void Dispose()
    {
        //dispose stuff goes here
    }
}
```

Usage

The following code snippet describes the client code of a generic class declared with the interface constraint:

```
private static void ImplementInterfaceConstraint()
{
    InterfaceConstraint<EntityClass> entityConstraint = new
InterfaceConstraint<EntityClass>();
    var result=entityConstraint.ImplementIt(new EntityClass {Name = "Gaurav
Aroraa"});
    WriteLine($"Name:{result.Name}");
}
```

In this section, we discussed generics and collections, including the various types of generics, and we also mentioned why we should use generics.

For more details on generics, visit the official documentation at `https://docs.microsoft.com/en-us/dotnet/csharp/programming-guide /generics/`.

Beautifying code using attributes

Attributes provide a way to associate information with code. This information could be as simple as a message/warning or can contain a complex operation or code itself. These are declared simply with the help of tags. These also help us to beautify our code by supplying inbuilt or custom attributes. Consider the following code:

```
private void PeerOperation()
{
    //other stuffs
    WriteLine("Level1 is completed.");
    //other stuffs
}
```

In this method, we show an informational message to notify the peer. The preceding method will be decorated with the help of an attribute. Consider the following code:

```
[PeerInformation("Level1 is completed.")]
private void PeerOperation()
{
    //other stuffs
}
```

Now, we can see that we just decorated our method with the help of an attribute.

According to the official documentation [`https://docs.microsoft.com/en-us/dotnet/csharp/tutorials/attributes`], attributes provide a way of associating information with code in a declarative way. They can also provide a reusable element that can be applied to a variety of targets.

Attributes can be used for the following:

- To add meta data information
- To add comments, description, compiler instructions, and so on

In the coming sections, we will discuss attributes in detail, with code examples.

Types of attributes

In the previous section, we discussed attributes, which help us to decorate and beautify our code. In this section, we will discuss the various types of attributes in detail.

AttributeUsage

This is a pre-defined attribute in a framework. This restricts the usage of attributes; in other words, it tells the type of items on which an attribute can be used, also known as attribute targets. These can be all or one of the following:

- Assembly
- Class
- Constructor
- Delegate
- Enum
- Event
- Field
- GenericParameter
- Interface
- Method
- Module

- Parameter
- Property
- ReturnValue
- Struct

By default, attributes are of any type of targets, unless you specify explicitly.

Example

The following attribute is created to be used only for a class:

```
[AttributeUsage(AttributeTargets.Class)]
public class PeerInformationAttribute : Attribute
{
    public PeerInformationAttribute(string information)
    {
        WriteLine(information);
    }
}
```

In preceding code, we defined attributes for the only use with class. If you try to use this attribute to other than class, then it will give you a compile-time error. See the following image, which shows an error for an attribute on method that is actually written solely for a class:

```
[PeerInformation("Level1 is completed.")]
0 references |
private vo        Attribute 'PeerInformation' is not valid on this declaration type. It is only valid on 'class' declarations.
{
    //othe        Attribute 'Day06.PeerInformationAttribute' is not valid on this declaration type. It is valid on 'Class' declarations only.
}
```

Obsolete

There may be circumstances when you want to raise a warning for a specific code so that it is conveyed on the client side. The Obsolete attribute is a predefined attribute that does the same and warns the calling user that a specific part is obsolete.

Example

Consider the following code snippet, which marks a class as `Obsolete`. You can compile and run the code even after a warning message because we have not asked this attribute to throw any error message on usage:

```
[Obsolete("Do not use this class use 'Person' instead.")]
public class Author:Person
{
    //other stuff goes here
}
```

The following image shows a warning message saying not to use the `Author` class, as it is `Obsolete`. But the client can still compile and run the code (we did not ask this attribute to throw error on usage):

```
0 references | Gaurav Arora, 1 day ago | 1 author, 1 change
private static void ImplementBaseClassConstraint()
{
    BaseClassConstraint<Author>baseClassConstraint = new BaseClassConstraint<Author>();
    var result = baseClassConstraint.ImplementIt(new Author
    {
        FirstName = "Shivprasad",          'Author' is obsolete: 'Do not use this class use 'Person' instead.'
        LastName = "Koirala",
        Age = 40                           Class 'Day06.Author' is obsolete: "Do not use this class use \'Person\' instead."
    });
                                           Show potential fixes (Ctrl+.)
    WriteLine($"Name:{result.FirstName} {result.LastName}");
    WriteLine($"Age:{result.Age}");
}
```

The following will throw an error message on usage along with the warning message:

```
[Obsolete("Do not use this class use 'Person' instead.",true)]
public class Author:Person
{
    //other stuff goes here
}
```

Consider the following image, where the user gets an exception after using the attribute, which is written to throw an error on usage:

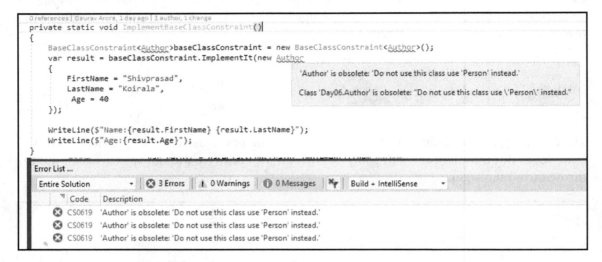

Conditional

The conditional attribute that is a predefined attribute, restricts the execution on the basis of condition applied to the code that is being processed.

Example

Consider the following code snippet, which restricts the conditional execution of a method for a defined debug preprocessor (we will discuss preprocessors in detail in the coming section):

```
#define Debug
using System.Diagnostics;
using static System.Console;

namespace Day06
{
    internal class Program
    {
        private static void Main(string[] args)
        {
            PersonList();
            ReadLine();
        }
```

```
        [Conditional("Debug")]
        private static void PersonList()
        {
            WriteLine("Person list:");
            foreach (var person in Person.GetPersonList())
            {
                WriteLine($"Name:{person.FirstName} {person.LastName}");
                WriteLine($"Age:{person.Age}");
            }
        }
    }
}
```

Remember one thing while defining preprocessor symbols; you define it on the very first line of the file.

Creating and implementing a custom attribute

In the previous section, we discussed the available or predefined attributes and we noticed that these are very limited, and in a real-world application, our requirements will demand more complex attributes. In such a case, we can create our own custom attributes; these attributes are similar to predefined attributes but with our custom operational code and target types. All custom attributes should be inherited from the System.Attribute class.

In this section, we will create a simple custom attribute as per the following requirements:

- Create an ErrorLogger attribute
- This attribute will handle all the available environments, that is, debug, development, production, and so on
- This method should be restricted only for methods
- It should show custom or supplied exception/exception messages
- By default, it should consider the environment as DEBUG
- It should show and throw exceptions if decorated for the development and DEBUG environment

Prerequisites

To create and run custom attributes, we should have the following prerequisites:

1. Visual Studio 2017 or later
2. .NET Core 1.1 or later

Here is the code snippet that creates our expected attribute:

```
public class ErrorLogger : Attribute
{
    public ErrorLogger(string exception)
    {
        switch (Env)
        {
            case Env.Debug:
            case Env.Dev:
                WriteLine($"{exception}");
                throw new Exception(exception);
            case Env.Prod:
                WriteLine($"{exception}");
                break;
            default:
                WriteLine($"{exception}");
                throw new Exception(exception);
        }
    }


    public Env Env { get; set; }
}
```

In the preceding code, we simply write to console whatever exceptions are supplied from the client code. In the case of the DEBUG or Dev environment, the exception is thrown further.

The following code snippet shows the simple usage of this attribute:

```
public class MathClass
{
    [ErrorLogger("Add Math opetaion in development", Env =
    Env.Debug)]
    public string Add(int num1, int num2)
    {
        return $"Sum of {num1} and {num2} = {num1 + num2}";
    }

    [ErrorLogger("Substract Math opetaion in development", Env =
    Env.Dev)]
    public string Substract(int num1, int num2)
    {
        return $"Substracrion of {num1} and {num2} = {num1 -
        num2}";
    }
```

```
    [ErrorLogger("Multiply Math opetaion in development", Env =
    Env.Prod)]
    public string Multiply(int num1, int num2)
    {
        return $"Multiplication of {num1} and {num2} = {num1 -
        num2}";
    }
}
```

In the preceding code, we have different methods that are marked for different environments. Out attributes will trigger and write the exceptions supplied for individual methods.

Leveraging preprocessor directives

As is clear from the name, preprocessor directives are the processes undertaken before the actual compilation starts. In other words, these preprocessors give instructions to the compiler to preprocess the information, and this works before the compiler compiles the code.

Important points

There are the following points to note for preprocessors while you're working with them:

- Preprocessor directives are actually conditions for the compiler
- Preprocessor directives must start with the # symbol
- Preprocessor directives should not be terminated with a semi colon (;) like a statement terminates
- Preprocessors are not used to create macros
- Preprocessors should be declared line by line

Preprocessor directives in action

Consider the following preprocessor directive:

```
#if ... #endif
```

This directive is a conditional directive, code executes whenever this directive is applied to the code, you can also use #elseif and/or #else directives. As this is a conditional directive and #if condition in C# is Boolean, these operators can be applied to check equality (==) and inequality (!=), and between multiple symbols, and (&&), or (||), and not (!) operators could also be applied to evaluate the condition.

 You should define a symbol on the very first line of the file where it is being applied with the use of #define.

Consider the following code snippet, which lets us know the conditional compilation:

```
#define DEBUG
#define DEV
using static System.Console;

namespace Day06
{
    public class PreprocessorDirective
    {
        public void ConditionalProcessor() =>
        #if (DEBUG && !DEV)
            WriteLine("Symbol is DEBUG.");
            #elseif (!DEBUG && DEV)
            WriteLine("Symbol is DEV");
            #else
            WriteLine("Symbols are DEBUG & DEV");
            #endif
    }
}
```

In the preceding code snippet, we have defined two variables for two different compilation environments, that is, DEBUG and DEV, and now, on the basis of our condition the following will be the output of the preceding code.

Symbols are DEBUG & DEV

#define and #undef

The #define directive basically defines a symbol for us that would be used in a conditional pre-processor directive.

#define cannot be used to declare constant values.

The following should be kept in mind while declaring a symbol with the use of #define:

- It cannot be used to declare constant
- It can define a symbol but cannot assign a value to these symbols
- Any instructions on the symbol should come after its definition of the symbol in the file that means #define directive always come before its usage
- Scope of the symbol defined or created with the help of #define directive is within the file where it is declared/defined

Recall the code example we discussed in the #if directive where we defined two symbols. So, it's very easy to define a symbol like: #define DEBUG.

The #undef directive lets us undefine the earlier defined symbol. This pre-processor should come before any non-directive statement. Consider the following code:

```
#define DEBUG
#define DEV
#undef DEBUG
using static System.Console;

namespace Day06
{
    public class PreprocessorDirective
    {
        public void ConditionalProcessor() =>
#if (DEBUG && !DEV)
            WriteLine("Symbol is DEBUG.");
#elif (!DEBUG && DEV)
            WriteLine("Symbol is DEV");
#else
            WriteLine("Symbols are DEBUG & DEV");
#endif
    }
}
```

In the preceding code, we are undefining the DEBUG symbol and the code will produce the following output:

The #region and #endregion directives

These directives are very helpful while working with long code-based files. Sometimes, while we are working on a long code base, let's say, an enterprise application, this kind of application will have 1000 lines of code and these lines will be part of different functions/methods or business logics. So, for better readability, we can manage these sections within the region. In a region, we can name and give short descriptions of the code that the region holds. Let's consider the following image:

```
1    #define DEBUG
2    #define DEV
3    #undef DEBUG
4    using static System.Console;
5
6  ⊟namespace Day06
7    {
        1 reference | 0 changes | 0 authors, 0 changes
8  ⊟    public class PreprocessorDirective
9        {
10 ⊟        #region  Conditional Pre-processor code
11
           1 reference | 0 changes | 0 authors, 0 changes
12 ⊟        public void ConditionalProcessor() =>
13 #if (DEBUG && !DEV)
14             WriteLine("Symbol is DEBUG.");
15 #elif (!DEBUG && DEV)
16             WriteLine("Symbol is DEV");
17 #else
18             WriteLine("Symbols are DEBUG & DEV");
19 #endif
20
21         #endregion
22     }
23 }
```

```
1    #define DEBUG
2    #define DEV
3    #undef DEBUG
4    using static System.Console;
5
6  ⊟namespace Day06
7    {
        1 reference | 0 changes | 0 authors, 0 changes
8  ⊟    public class PreprocessorDirective
9        {
10 ⊞        Conditional Pre-processor code
22     }
23 }
```

```
#region  Conditional Pre-processor code

       public void ConditionalProcessor() =>
#if (DEBUG && !DEV)
           WriteLine("Symbol is DEBUG.");
#elif (!DEBUG && DEV)
           WriteLine("Symbol is DEV");
#else
           WriteLine("Symbols are DEBUG & DEV");
#endif
```

In the preceding image, the left-hand side portion shows the expanded view of the `#region` ... `#endregion` directives, which tells us how we can apply these directives to our long code base files. The right-hand side of the image shows the collapsed view, and when you hover the mouse on the collapsed region text, you can see that a rectangular block appears in Visual Studio, which says what all these regions contain. So, you need not expand the region to check what code is written under this region.

The #line directive

The `#line` directive provides a way to modify the actual line number of compilers. You can also provide the output `FileName` for errors and warnings, which is optional. This directive may be useful in automated intermediate steps in the build process. In scenarios where the line numbers have been removed from the original source code, however you would require to generate the output based on the original file with numbering.

Additionally, the `#line` default directive returns the line numbering to its default value, and it counts a line where it was renumbered earlier.

The `#line` hidden directive does not affect the filename or line numbers in error reporting.

The `#line` filename directive profiles a way to name a file you want to appear in the compiler output. In this, the default value is the actual filename in use; you can provide a new name in double quotes, and this must be preceded by the line number.

Consider the following code snippet:

```
public void LinePreprocessor()
{
    #line 85 "LineprocessorIsTheFileName"
    WriteLine("This statement is at line#85 and not at
    line# 25");
    #line default
    WriteLine("This statement is at line#29 and not at
    line# 28");
    #line hidden
    WriteLine("This statement is at line#30");
}
}
```

In the preceding code snippet, we marked our line number 85 for the first statement, which was originally at line number 25.

The #warning directive

The #warning directive provides a way to generate a warning in any part of code and usually work within the conditional directives. Consider the following code snippet:

```
public void WarningPreProcessor()
{
    #if DEBUG
    #warning "This is a DEBUG compilation."
    WriteLine("Environment is DEBUG.");
    #endif
}
}
```

The preceding code will warn at compile time, and the warning message will be what you provided with the #warning directive:

```
                1 reference | 0 changes | 0 authors, 0 changes
                public void WarningPreProcessor()
                {
#if DEBUG
#warning "This is a DEBUG compilation."
                    WriteLine("Enviror       i
#endif                                            #warning: '"This is a DEBUG compilation."'
                }
                }                                 Show potential fixes (Ctrl+.)
```

#error

The #error directive provides a way to generate an error in any part of code. Consider the following code snippet:

```
public void ErrorPreProcessor()
{
    #if DEV
    #error "This is a DEV compilation."
    WriteLine("Environment is DEV.");
    #endif
}
```

This will throw an error, and due to this error your code will not be built properly; it fails the build with the error message that you provided with `#error` directive. Let's have a look at the following image:

```
    0 references | 0 changes | 0 authors, 0 changes
        public void ErrorPreProcessor()
        {
#if DEV
#error "This is a DEV compilation."
            WriteLine("Environment :
                                        #error: '"This is a DEV compilation."'
#endif
        }
```

In this section, we discussed all about preprocessor directives and their usage with code examples.

For a complete reference of C# preprocessor directives, please refer to the official documentation:
`https://docs.microsoft.com/en-us/dotnet/csharp/language-reference/preprocessor-directives/`

Getting started with LINQ

LINQ is nothing but an acronym of Language Integrated Query that is part of programming language. LINQ provides an easy way to write or query data with a specified syntax like we would use the where clause when trying to query data for some specific criteria. So, we can say that LINQ is a syntax that is used to query data.

In this section, we will see a simple example to query data. We have `Person` list and the following code snippet provides us a various way to query data:

```csharp
private static void TestLINQ()
{
    var person = from p in Person.GetPersonList()
        where p.Id == 1
        select p;
    foreach (var per in person)
    {
        WriteLine($"Person Id:{per.Id}");
        WriteLine($"Name:{per.FirstName} {per.LastName}");
        WriteLine($"Age:{per.Age}");
    }
}
```

In the preceding code snippet, we are querying `List` of persons for *personId* =1. The LINQ query returns a result of `IEnumerable<Person>` type which can be easily accessed using `foreach`. This code produces the following output:

```
Person Id:1
Name:Denim Pinto
Age:31
```

 Complete discussion of LINQ is beyond the scope of this book. For complete LINQ functionality refer to: `https://code.msdn.microsoft.com/101-LINQ-Samples-3fb9811b`

Writing unsafe code

In this section, we will discuss introduction to how to write unsafe code using Visual Studio. Language C# provides a way to write code which compiles and creates the objects and these objects under the root are managed by the garbage collector [refer to `day 01` for more details on garbage collector]. In simple words, C# is not like C, C++ language which use concept of function pointer to access references. But there is a situation when it is necessary to use function-pointers in C# language similar to languages that support function-pointers like C or C++ but C# language does not support it. To overcome such situations, we have unsafe code in C# language. There is modifier unsafe which tells that this code is not controlled by Garbage collector and within that block we can use function pointers and other unsafe stuffs. To use unsafe code, we first inform compiler to set on unsafe compilation from Visual Studio 2017 or later just go to project properties and on **Build** tab, select the option **Allow unsafe code**, refer following screenshot:

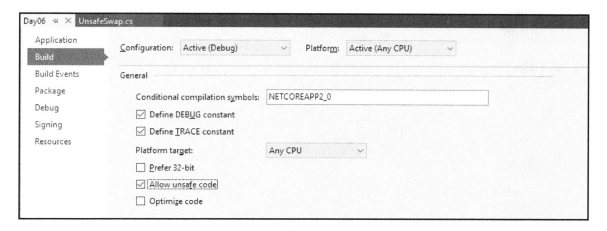

You would not be able to continue with unsafe code if this option is not selected, please refer following screenshot:

```
 1  namespace Day06
 2  {
 3      public  class UnsafeSwap
 4      {
 5
 6          public unsafe void SwapNumbers(int*  num1, int* num2)
 7          {
 8                                         Unsafe code may only appear if compiling with /unsafe
 9          }
10      }
11  }
```

After setting unsafe compilation, let's write code to swap two numbers using pointers, consider the following code snippet:

```
public unsafe void SwapNumbers(int*  num1, int* num2)
{
    int tempNum = *num1;
    *num1 = *num2;
    *num2 = tempNum;
}
```

Previous is a very simple swap function which is just swapping two numbers with the help of pointers. Let's make a call to this function to see the actual results:

```
private static unsafe void TestUnsafeSwap()
{
    Write("Enter first number:");
    var num1 = Convert.ToInt32(ReadLine());
    Write("Enter second number:");
    var num2 = Convert.ToInt32(ReadLine());
    WriteLine("Before calling swap function:");
    WriteLine($"Number1:{num1}, Number2:{num2}");
    //call swap
    new UnsafeSwap().SwapNumbers(&num1, &num2);
    WriteLine("After calling swap function:");
    WriteLine($"Number1:{num1}, Number2:{num2}");
}
```

In the preceding code snippet, we are taking input of two numbers and then showing the results before and after swaps, this produces the following output:

```
Enter first number:55
Enter second number:189
Before calling swap function:
Number1:55, Number2:189
After calling swap function:
Number1:189, Number2:55
```

In this section, we have discussed how to deal with unsafe code.

 For more details on unsafe code, refer to official documentations of language specifications: https://docs.microsoft.com/en-us/dotnet/csharp/language-reference/language-specification/unsafe-code

Writing asynchronous code

Before we discuss the code in async way, lets first discuss our normal code that is nothing but a synchronous code, let's consider following code snippet:

```
public class FilePolling
{
    public void PoleAFile(string fileName)
    {
```

```
        Console.Write($"This is polling file:
        {fileName}");
        //file polling stuff goes here
    }
}
```

The preceding code snippet is short and sweet. It tells us it is polling to a specific file. Here system has to wait to complete the operation of poling a file before it start next. This is what synchronous code is. Now, consider a scenario where we need not wait to complete the operation of this function to start another operation or function. To meet such scenarios, we have asynchronous coding, this is possible with the keyword, **async**.

Consider following code:

```
public async void PoleAFileAsync(string fileName)
{
    Console.Write($"This is polling file: {fileName}");
    //file polling async stuff goes here
}
```

Just with the help of the `async` keyword our code is able to make asynchronous calls.

In the view of previous code we can say that asynchronous programming is one that let not wait client code to execute another function or operation during any async operation. In simple word, we can say that asynchronous code can't hold another operation that need to be called.

In this chapter, we discussed asynchronous coding. A complete discussion on this topic is beyond the scope of our book. For complete details refer to official documentation: `https:/ /docs.microsoft.com/en-us/dotnet/csharp/async`

Hands-on exercises

1. Define generic classes by creating generic code of `StringCalculator`: `https:// github.com/garora/TDD-Katas/tree/develop/Src/cs/StringCalculator`
2. Create a generic and non-generic collection and test which one is better as per performance.
3. We have discussed code snippets in the section-*Why one should use Generics?* that tells about run-time compilation exceptions. In this regard, why should we not use the same code in the following way?

```
    internal class Program
    {
```

```
        private static void Main(string[] args)
{
        //No exception at compile-time or run-time
        ArrayList authorEditorArrayList = new ArrayList {
        "Gaurav Arora", 43, "Vikas Tiwari", 25 };
        foreach (var authorEditor in authorEditorArrayList)
        {
            WriteLine($"{authorEditor}");
        }
    }
}
```

1. What is the use of the `default` keyword in generic code, elaborate with the help of a real-world example.
2. Write simple code by using all 3-types of predefined attributes.
3. What is the default restriction type for an attribute? Write a program to showcase all restriction types.
4. Create a custom attribute with name - *LogFailuresAttribute* that log all exceptions in a text file.
5. Why pre-processor directive `#define` cannot be used to declare constant values?
6. Write a program to create a `List` of `Authors` and apply LINQ functionality on it.
7. Write a program to sort an array
8. Write a complete program to write a sync and async methods to write a file.

Revisiting Day 6

Today, we discussed advanced concepts such as generics, attributes, preprocessors, LINQ, unsafe code, and asynchronous programming.

Our day started with generics, where you learned about generic classes with the help of code snippets. Then, we dived into attributes and learned how to decorate our C# code with predefined attributes. We have created one custom attribute and used it in our code example. We discussed preprocessor directives with complete examples and learned the usage of these directives in our coding. Other concepts discussed are LINQ, unsafe code, and asynchronous programming.

Tomorrow, that is, day seven will be the concluding day of our seven-day learning series. We will cover OOP concepts and their implementation in the C# language.

7

Day 07 - Understanding Object-Oriented Programming with C#

Today we are on day seven of our seven-day learning series. Yesterday (day six), we went through a few advanced topics and we discussed attributes, generics, and LINQ. Today, we will start learning **object-oriented programming** (**OOP**) using C#.

This will be a practical approach to OOP, while covering all the aspects. You will benefit even without having any basic knowledge of OOP and move on to confidently practicing this easily in the workplace.

We will be covering these topics:

- Introduction to OOP
- Discussing object relationships
- Encapsulation
- Abstraction
- Inheritance
- Polymorphism

Introduction to OOP

OOP is one of the programming paradigms that is purely based on objects. These objects contain data (please refer to day sevenfor more details).

When we do the classification of programming languages it is called programming paradigm. For more information refer to `https://en.wikipedia.org/wiki/Programming_paradigm`.

OOP has come into consideration to overcome the limitations of earlier programming approaches (consider the procedural language approach).

Generally, I define OOP as follows:

A modern programming language in which we use objects as building blocks to develop applications.

There are a lot of examples of objects in our surroundings and in the real world, we have various aspects that are the representation of objects. Let us go back to our programming world and think about a program that is defined as follows:

A program is a list of instructions that instructs the language compiler on what to do.

To understand OOP more closely, we should know about earlier programming approaches, mainly procedural programming, structured programming, and so on.

- **Structured programming**: This is a term coined by Edsger W. Dijkstra in 1966. Structured programming is a programming paradigm that solves a problem to handle 1000 lines of code and divides these into small parts. These small parts are mostly called subroutine, block structures, `for` and `while` loops, and so on. Known languages that use structured programming techniques are ALGOL, Pascal, PL/I, and so on.
- **Procedural programming**: A paradigm derived from structured programming and simply based on how we make a call (known as a procedural call). Known languages that use procedural programming techniques are COBOL, Pascal, C. A recent example of the Go programming language was published in 2009.

The main problem with these two approaches is that programs are not well manageable once they grow. Programs with more complex and large code bases make these two approaches strained. In short, the maintainability of the code is tedious with the use of these two approaches. To overcome such problems now, we have OOP, which has the following features:

- Inheritance
- Encapsulation
- Polymorphism
- Abstraction

Discussing Object relations

Before we start our discussion on OOP, first we should understand relationships. In the real world, objects have relationships between them and hierarchies as well. There are the following types of relationships in object-oriented programming:

- **Association**: Association represents a relationship between objects in a manner that all objects have their own life cycle. In association, there is no owner of these objects. For example, a person in a meeting. Here, the person and the meeting are independent; there is no parent of them. A person can have multiple meetings and a meeting can combine multiple persons. The meeting and persons are both independently initialized and destroyed.

 Aggregation and composition are both types of association.

- **Aggregation**: Aggregation is a specialized form of association. Similar to association, objects have their own life cycle in aggregations, but it involves ownership that means a child object cannot belong to another parent object. Aggregation is a one-way relationship where the lives of objects are independent from each other. For example, the child and parent relationship is an aggregation, because every child has parent but it's not necessary that every parent has child.
- **Composition**: Composition is a relationship of *death* that represents the relationship between two objects and one object (child) depends on another object (parent). If the parent object is deleted, all its children automatically get deleted. For example, a house and a room. One house has multiple rooms. But a single room cannot belong to multiple houses. If we demolished the house, the room would automatically delete.

In the coming sections, we will discuss all features of OOP in detail. Also, we will understand implementing these features using C#.

Inheritance

Inheritance is one of the most important features/concepts of OOP. It is self-explanatory in name; inheritance inherits features from a class. In simple words, inheritance is an activity performed at compile-time as instructed with the help of the syntax. The class that inherits another class is known as the child or derived class, and the class which is being inherited is known as the base or parent class. Here, derived classes inherit all the features of base classes either to implement or to override.

In the coming sections, we will discuss inheritance in detail with code examples using C#.

Understanding inheritance

Inheritance as a feature of OOP helps you to define a child class. This child class inherits the behavior of the parent or base class.

 Inheriting a class means reusing the class. In C#, inheritance is symbolically defined using the colon (:) sign.

The modifier (refer to `Chapter 2`, *Day 02 - Getting Started with C#*) tells us what the scope of the reuse of the base class for derived classes is. For instance, consider that class *B* inherits class *A*. Here, class *B* contains all the features of class *A* including its own features. Refer the following diagram:

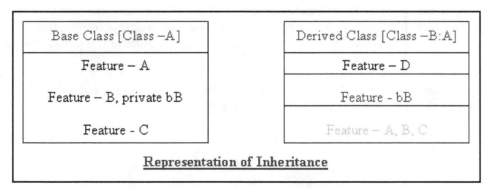

Base Class [Class –A]	Derived Class [Class –B:A]
Feature – A	Feature – D
Feature – B, private bB	Feature - bB
Feature - C	Feature – A, B, C

Representation of Inheritance

In the preceding figure, the derived class (that is, *B*) inherits all the features by ignoring modifiers. Features are inherited whether these are public or private. These modifiers come in to consideration when these features are going to be implemented. At the time of implementation only public features are considered. So, here, public features, that is, *A*, *B*, and *C* will be implemented but private features, that is, *B*, will not be implemented.

Types of inheritance

Up until this point, we have got the idea about inheritance. Now, it's time to discuss inheritance types; inheritance is of the following types:

- **Single inheritance:**

    This is a widely used type of inheritance. Single inheritance is when a class inherits another class. A class that inherits another class is called a child class and the class which is being inherited is called a parent or base class. In the child class, the class inherits features from one parent class only.

     C# only supports single inheritance.

    You can inherit classes hierarchically (as we will see in the following section), but that is a single inheritance in nature for a derived class. Refer the following diagram:

Base Class [Class –A]	Derived Class [Class –B:A]
Feature – A	Feature – D
Feature – B	Feature – A, B, C
Feature - C	

Representation of Single Inheritance

The preceding diagram is a representation of a single inheritance that shows *Class B* (inherited class) inheriting *Class A* (base class). *Class B* can reuse all features that is, *A, B,* and *C,* including its own feature, that is, D. Visibility or reusability of members in inheritance depends on the protection levels (this will be discussed in the coming section, *Member visibility in inheritance*).

- **Multiple inheritance:**

  Multiple inheritance happens when a derived class inherits multiple base classes. Languages such as C++ support multiple inheritance. C# does not support multiple inheritance, but we can achieve multiple inheritance with the help of interfaces. If you are curious to know that why C# does not support multiple inheritance, refer to this official link at `https://blogs.msdn.microsoft.com/csharpfaq/2004/03/07/why-doesnt-c-support-multiple-inheritance/`. Refer to the following diagram:

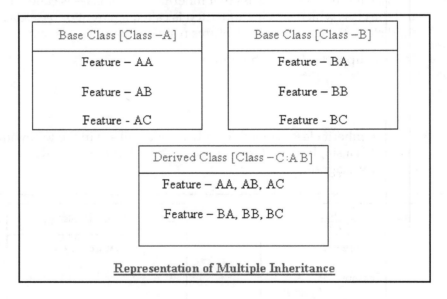

Representation of Multiple Inheritance

The preceding diagram is a representation of multiple inheritance (not possible in C# without the help of interfaces), which shows that *Class C* (derived class) inherits from two base classes (*A* and *B*). In multiple inheritance, the derived *Class C* will have all the features of both *Class A* and *Class B*.

- **Hierarchical inheritance:**

  Hierarchical inheritance happens when more than one class inherits from one class. Refer to the following diagram:

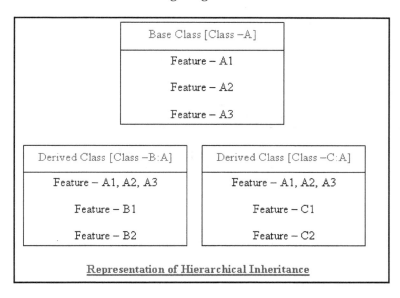

Representation of Hierarchical Inheritance

  In the preceding diagram, *Class B* (derived class) and *Class C* (derived class) inherit from *Class A* (base class). With the help of hierarchical inheritance, *Class B* can use all the features of *Class A*. Similarly, *Class C* can also use all the features of *Class A*.

- **Multilevel inheritance:**

  When a class is derived from a class that is already a derived class, it is called multilevel inheritance.

 In multi-level inheritance, the recently derived class owns the features of all the earlier derived classes.

In this, a derived class can have its parent and a parent of the parent class. Refer to the following diagram:

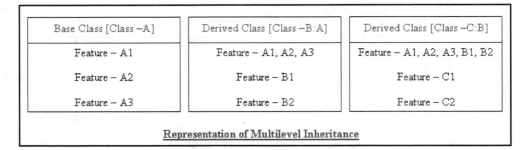

Base Class [Class –A]	Derived Class [Class –B:A]	Derived Class [Class –C:B]
Feature – A1	Feature – A1, A2, A3	Feature – A1, A2, A3, B1, B2
Feature – A2	Feature – B1	Feature – C1
Feature – A3	Feature – B2	Feature – C2

<u>**Representation of Multilevel Inheritance**</u>

The preceding diagram represents multilevel inheritance and shows that *Class C* (recently derived class) can reuse all the features of *Class B* and *Class A*.

- **Hybrid inheritance:**

    Hybrid inheritance is a combination of more than one inheritance.

 C# does not support hybrid inheritance.

Combination of multiple and multilevel inheritance is a hierarchical inheritance, where a parent class is a derived class and a recently derived class inherits multiple parent classes. There can be more combinations. Refer to the following diagram:

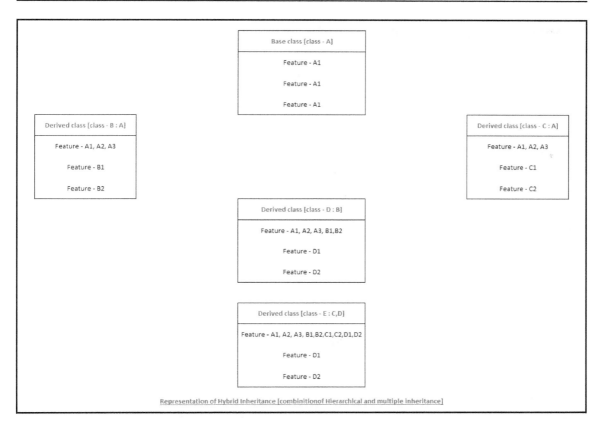

Representation of Hybrid Inheritance [combinition of Hierarchical and multiple inheritance]

The preceding image, representing hybrid inheritance, shows the combination hierarchical and multiple inheritance. You can see that *Class A* is a parent class and all the other classes are derived from *Class A*, directly or indirectly. Our derived *Class E* can reuse all the features of Class *A, B, C,* and *D*.

- **Implicit inheritance:**

    All the types in .NET implicitly inherit from `system.object` or its derived classes. For more information on implicit inheritance, refer to `https://docs.microsoft.com/en-us/dotnet/csharp/tutorials/inheritance#implicit-inheritance`.

Member visibility in inheritance

As we discussed earlier, in inheritance, derived classes can reuse the functionality of the parent class and use or modify the members of its parent class. But these members can be reused or modified as per their access modifier or visibility (for more details refer to `Chapter 4`, *Day 04 - Discussing C# Class Members*).

In this section, we will briefly discuss member visibility in inheritance. In any type of inheritance (that is possible in C# language) the following members cannot be inherited by base classes:

- **Static constructors**: A static constructor is one that initializes the static data (refer to the *Modifier* section of `Chapter 4`, *Day 04: Discussing C# Class Members*). The importance of static constructors is that these are called before the creation of the first instance of a class or any other static members called or referred to in some operations. Being a static data initializer, a static constructor cannot be inherited by a derived class.
- **Instance constructor**: It is not a static constructor; whenever you create a new instance of a class, a constructor is called, which is the instance class. A class can have multiple constructors. As the instance constructor is used to create an instance of a class, it is not inherited by the derived class. For more information on constructors, refer to `https://docs.microsoft.com/en-us/dotnet/csharp/programming-guide/classes-and-structs/constructors`.
- **Finalizers**: These are just destructors of classes. These are used or called by garbage collectors at runtime to destroy the instances of a class. As finalizers are called only once and are per class, these cannot be inherited by a derived class. For more information on destructors or finalizers, refer to `https://docs.microsoft.com/en-us/dotnet/csharp/programming-guide/classes-and-structs/destructors`.

Derived classes can reuse or inherit all the members of the base class, but their usage or visibility depends upon their access modifiers (refer to `Chapter 4`, *Day 04 - Discussing C# Class Members*). Different visibility of these members depends upon the following accessibility modifiers:

- **Private**: If a member is `private`, the visibility of a `private` member is restricted to its derived class; `private` members are available in derived classes if the derived class nests to its base class.

Consider the following code snippet:

```
public class BaseClass
{
    private const string AuthorName = "Gaurav Aroraa";
    public class DeriveClass: BaseClass
    {
        public void Display()
        {
            Write("This is from inherited Private member:");
            WriteLine($"{nameof(AuthorName)}'{AuthorName}'");
            ReadLine();
        }
    }
}
```

In the preceding code snippet, BaseClass is to have one private member, AuthorName, and this will be available in DeriveClass, as DeriveClass is a nested class of BaseClass. You can also see this in compile time while moving the cursor over to the usage of the private AuthorName member. See the following screenshot:

The preceding image shows the visibility of a private method for a derived class. The private method is visible in the derived class if the class is nested within its base class.

If the class is not nested within its parent/base class, then you can see the following compile-time exception:

```
0 references | 0 changes | 0 authors, 0 changes
public class ChildClass : BaseClass
{
    0 references | 0 changes | 0 authors, 0 changes
    public void Display()
    {
        Write("This inherited Private member is not visible here:");
        WriteLine($"{nameof(AuthorName)}'{AuthorName}'");
        ReadLine();
    }                           'BaseClass.AuthorName' is inaccessible due to its protection level
}
                                Cannot access private constant 'AuthorName' here

                                Show potential fixes (Ctrl+.)
```

In the preceding screenshot, we have `ChildClass`, which inherits from `BaseClass`. Here, we cannot use private members of `BaseClass` as `ChildClass` is not nested within `BaseClass`.

- **Protected**: If a member is a protected modifier, it is only visible to the derived class. These members will not be available or visible while you're using the using the instance of a base class, because these are defined as protected.

The following screenshot depicts how a protected member can be accessible/visible using the base class:

```
0 references | 0 changes | 0 authors, 0 changes
public class ChildClass : BaseClass
{
    0 references | 0 changes | 0 authors, 0 changes
    public void Display()
    {
        Write("This inherited Protected member is visible here:");
        WriteLine($"{nameof(EditorName)}'{EditorName}'");
        ReadLine();                 □, (constant) string BaseClass.EditorName = "Vikas Tiwari"
    }
}
```

In the preceding screenshot, the protected member, `EditorName` is visible in `ChildClass` because it inherits `BaseClass`.

The following screenshot shows that the protected members are not accessible using the instance of `BaseClass` in `ChildClass`. If you try to do so, you will get a compile-time error:

```
0 references | 0 changes | 0 authors, 0 changes
public class ChildClass : BaseClass
{
    0 references | 0 changes | 0 authors, 0 changes
    public void Display()
    {
        BaseClass baseClass = new BaseClass();
        Write("This Protected member is not visible here:");
        WriteLine($"{nameof(baseClass.EditorName)}'{baseClass.EditorName}'");

        ReadLine();          Cannot access protected member 'BaseClass.EditorName' via a qualifier of type 'BaseClass'; the qualifier must be of type 'ChildClass' (or derived from it)
    }
}                            Cannot access protected field 'EditorName' here
```

- **Internal**: Members with internal modifiers are only available in the derived classes of the same assembly as of the base class. These members can't be available for derived classes that belong to other assemblies.

  Consider the following code-snippet:

  ```csharp
  namespace Day07
  {
      public class MemberVisibility
      {
          private void InternalMemberExample()
          {
              var childClass = new Lib.ChildClass();
              WriteLine("Calling from derived class that
              belongs to same assembly of BaseClass");
              childClass.Display();
          }
      }
  }
  ```

  The preceding code shows the visibility of an internal member. Here, `ChildClass` belongs to the `Lib` assembly, which is where `BaseClass` exists.

On the other hand, if `BaseClass` exists in an assembly other than `Lib`, then internal members will not accessible; see the following screenshot:

```
0 references | 0 changes | 0 authors, 0 changes
public class ChilClassofExternalBaseClass : Lib.BaseClass
{
    0 references | 0 changes | 0 authors, 0 changes
    public void Display()
    {
        Write("This internal members of Lib.BaseClass is not visible here:");
        WriteLine($"{nameof(ReviewerName)} is '{ReviewerName}'");
    }
}
```

'BaseClass.ReviewerName' is inaccessible due to its protection level

Cannot access internal field 'ReviewerName' here

The preceding screenshot shows a compile-time error that tells that the internal members are inaccessible, as they are not available in the same assembly.

- **Public**: Public members are available or visible in derived classes and can be used further.

Consider the following code-snippet:

```
public class ChilClassYounger : ChildClass
{
    private string _copyEditor = "Diwakar Shukla";
    public new void Display()
    {
        WriteLine($"This is from ChildClassYounger: copy
        editor is '{_copyEditor}'");
        WriteLine("This is from ChildClass:");
        base.Display();
    }
}
```

In the preceding code snippet, `ChildClassYoung` has a `Display()` method that displays the console output. `ChildClass` also has a public `Display()` method that also displays the console output. In our derived class, we can reuse the `Display()` method of `ChildClass` because it is declared as public. After running the previous code, it will give the following output:

```
Day 07: Learning C# in 7-days
Member visibility
This is from ChildClassYounger: copy editor is 'Diwakar Shukla'
This is from ChildClass:
This Protected member is visible here:EditorName is 'Vikas Tiwari'
```

In the previous code, you should notice that we added a `new` keyword with the `Display()` method of the `ChildClassYounger` class. This is because we have a method with the same name in the parent class (that is, `ChildClass`). If we don't add the `new` keyword, we'll see a compile-time warning, as shown in the following screenshot:

```
2 references | 0 changes | 0 authors, 0 changes
public class ChilClassYounger : ChildClass
{
    private string _copyEditor = "Diwakar Shukla";

    1 reference | 0 changes | 0 authors, 0 changes
    public void Display()
    {
        WriteLine(s T    'ChilClassYounger.Display()' hides inherited member 'ChildClass.Display()'. Use the new keyword if hiding was intended.
        WriteLine("Th
        base.Display('    The keyword 'new' is required on 'Display' because it hides method 'void Day07.ChildClass.Display()'
    }
                        Show potential fixes (Ctrl+.)
}
```

By applying the `new` keyword, you hide the `ChildClass.Display()` member that is inherited from `ChildClass`. In C#, this concept is called method hiding.

Implementing inheritance

In the previous section, you learned about inheritance in detail and went through its various types. You also learned inherited member's visibility. In this section, we will implement inheritance.

Inheritance is representation of an **IS-A** relation, which suggests that `Author` **IS-A** `Person` and `Person` **IS-A** `Human`, so `Author` **IS-A** `Human`. Let's understand this in a code example:

```
public class Person
{
    public string FirstName { get; set; } = "Gaurav";
    public string LastName { get; set; } = "Aroraa";
    public int Age { get; set; } = 43;
    public string Name => $"{FirstName} {LastName}";
    public virtual void Detail()
```

```
    {
        WriteLine("Person's Detail:");
        WriteLine($"Name: {Name}");
        WriteLine($"Age: {Age}");
        ReadLine();
    }
}
public class Author:Person
{
    public override void Detail()
    {
        WriteLine("Author's detail:");
        WriteLine($"Name: {Name}");
        WriteLine($"Age: {Age}");
        ReadLine();
    }
}
public class Editor : Person
{
    public override void Detail()
    {
        WriteLine("Editor's detail:");
        WriteLine($"Name: {Name}");
        WriteLine($"Age: {Age}");
        ReadLine();
    }
}
public class Reviewer : Person
{
    public override void Detail()
    {
        WriteLine("Reviewer's detail:");
        WriteLine($"Name: {Name}");
        WriteLine($"Age: {Age}");
        ReadLine();
    }
}
```

In the preceding code, we have a base class, `Person` and three derived classes, namely `Author`, `Editor`, and `Reviewer`. This shows single inheritance. The following is the implementation of the previous code:

```
private static void InheritanceImplementationExample()
{
    WriteLine("Inheritance implementation");
    WriteLine();
    var person = new Person();
    WriteLine("Parent class Person:");
```

```
        person.Detail();
        var author = new Author();
        WriteLine("Derive class Author:");
        Write("First Name:");
        author.FirstName = ReadLine();
        Write("Last Name:");
        author.LastName = ReadLine();
        Write("Age:");
        author.Age = Convert.ToInt32(ReadLine());
        author.Detail();
        //code removed
    }
```

In the preceding code, we instantiated a single class and called details; each class inherits the Person class and, hence, all its members. This produces the following output:

```
Day 07: Learning C# in 7-days
Inheritance implementation

Parent class Person:
Person's Detail:
Name: Gaurav Aroraa
Age: 43

Derive class Author:
First Name:Gaurav
Last Name:Arora
Age:43
Author's detail:
Name: Gaurav Arora
Age: 43

Derive class Editor:
First Name:Vikas
Last Name:Tiwari
Age:25
Editor's detail:
Name: Vikas Tiwari
Age: 25

Derive class Reviewer:
First Name:Shivprasad
Last Name:Koirala
Age:40
Reviewer's detail:
Name: Shivprasad Koirala
Age: 40
```

Implementing multiple inheritance in C#

We have already discussed in the previous section that C# does not support multiple inheritance. But we can achieve multiple inheritance with the help of interfaces (refer to Chapter 2, *Day 02 – Getting Started with C#*). In this section, we will implement multiple inheritance using C#.

Let's consider the code snippet of the previous section, which implements single inheritance. Let's rewrite the code by implementing interfaces.

 Interfaces represent **Has-A/Can-Do** relationship, which indicates that Publisher **Has-A** Author and Author **Has-A** Book. In C#, you can assign an instance of a class to any variable that is of the type of the interface or the base class. In view of OOP, this concept is referred to as polymorphism (refer to the *Polymorphism* section for more details).

First of all, let's create an interface:

```
public interface IBook
{
    string Title { get; set; }
    string Isbn { get; set; }
    bool Ispublished { get; set; }
    void Detail();
}
```

In the preceding code snippet, we created an IBook interface, which is related to book details. This interface is intended to collect book details, such as Title, ISBN, and whether the book is published. It has a method that provides the complete book details.

Now, let's implement the IBook interface to derive the Author class, which inherits the Person class:

```
public class Author:Person, IBook
{
    public string Title { get; set; }
    public string Isbn { get; set; }
    public bool Ispublished { get; set; }
    public override void Detail()
    {
        WriteLine("Author's detail:");
        WriteLine($"Name: {Name}");
        WriteLine($"Age: {Age}");
        ReadLine();
    }
    void IBook.Detail()
```

```
    {
        WriteLine("Book details:");
        WriteLine($"Author Name: {Name}");
        WriteLine($"Author Age: {Age}");
        WriteLine($"Title: {Title}");
        WriteLine($"Isbn: {Isbn}");
        WriteLine($"Published: {(Ispublished ? "Yes" :
        "No")}");
        ReadLine();
    }
}
```

In the preceding code snippet, we implemented multiple inheritance with the use of the
`IBook` interface. Our derived class `Author` inherits the `Person` base class and implements
the `IBook` interface. In the preceding code, a notable point is that both the class and
interface have the `Detail()` method. Now, it depends on which method we want to
modify or which method we want to reuse. If we try to modify the `Detail()` method of the
`Person` class, then we need to override or hide it (using the `new` keyword). On the other
hand, if we want to use the interface's method, we need to explicitly call the
`IBook.Detail()` method. When you call interface methods explicitly, modifiers are not
required; hence, there is no need to put a `public` modifier here. This method implicitly has
public visibility:

```
//multiple Inheritance
WriteLine("Book details:");
Write("Title:");
author.Title = ReadLine();
Write("Isbn:");
author.Isbn = ReadLine();
Write("Published (Y/N):");
author.Ispublished = ReadLine() == "Y"; ((IBook)author).Detail(); //
we need to cast as both Person class and IBook has same named methods
```

The preceding code snippet calls the interface method; note how we are casting the instance of our `Author` class with `IBook`:

```
Day 07: Learning C# in 7-days
Inheritance implementation

Parent class Person:
Person's Detail:
Name: Gaurav Aroraa
Age: 43

Derive class Author:
First Name:Gaurav
Last Name:Arora
Age:43
Author's detail:
Name: Gaurav Arora
Age: 43

Book details:
Title:Learn C# in 7-days
Isbn:9781787287044
Published (Y/N):N
Book details:
Author Name: Gaurav Arora
Author Age: 43
Title: Learn C# in 7-days
Isbn: 9781787287044
Published: No
```

The preceding image shows the output of the implemented code using interfaces. All the members of the interface are accessible to the child class; there is no need for special implementation when you are instantiating a child class. The instance of a child class is able to access all the visible members. The important point in the preceding implementation is in the `((IBook)author).Detail();` statement, where we explicitly cast the instance of child class to the interface to get the implementation of the interface member. By default, it provides the implementation of a class member, so we need explicitly tell the compiler that we need an interface method.

Abstraction

Abstraction is the process where relevant data is shown by hiding irrelevant or unnecessary information. For example, if you purchase a mobile phone, you'd not be interested in the process of how your message is delivered or how your call connects another number, but you'd be interested to know that whenever you press the call button on your phone, it should connect your call. In this example, we hide those features that do not interest the user and provide those features that interest the user. This process is called abstraction.

Implementing abstraction

In C#, abstraction can be implemented with the use of:

Abstract class

Abstract class is half-defined that means it provides a way to override members to its child classes. We should use base classes in the project where we need have a need same member to all its child classes with own implementations or want to override. For an example if we have an abstract class Car with an abstract method color and have child classes HondCar, FordCar, MarutiCar etc. in this case all child classes would have color member but with different implementation because color method would be overridden in the child classes with their own implementations. The point to be noted here - abstract classes represent IS-A relation.

 You can also revisit our discussion of abstract class during Day04 section 'abstract' and code-examples to understand the implementation.

Features of abstract class

In previous section we learned about abstract classes, here are the few features of abstract class:

- Abstract class can't be initialized that means, you cannot create an object of abstract class.
- Abstract class is meant to act as a base class so, other classes can inherit it.

- If you declared an abstract class then by design it must be inherited by other classes.
- An abstract class can have both concrete or abstract methods. Abstrcat methods should be implemented in the child class that inherited abstract class.

Interface

An interface does not contain functionality or concrete members. You can call this is a contract for the class or structure that will implement to define the signatures of the functionality. With the use of interface, you make sure that whenever a class or struct implement it that class or struct is going to use the contract of the interface. For an instance if ICalculator interface has method Add() that means whenever a class or structure implement this interface it provides a specific contractual functionality that is addition.

 For more information on interface, refer: `https://docs.microsoft.com/en-us/dotnet/csharp/programming-guide/interfaces/index`

Interface can only have these members:

- Methods
- Properties
- Indexers
- Events

Features of interface

Followings are the main features of interfaces

- Interface is internal by default
- All member of interface is public by default and there is no need to explicitly apply public modifier to the members
- Similarly, to abstract class, interface also cannot be instantiated. They can only implement and the class or structure that implement it should implement all the members.
- Interface cannot contain any concrete method
- An interface can be implemented by another interface, a class or struct.
- A class or struct can implement multiple interfaces.

A class can inherit abstract class or a normal class and implement an interface.

In this section, we will implement abstraction using abstract class. Let's consider following code-snippet:

```
public class AbstractionImplementation
{
public void Display()
{
BookAuthor author = new BookAuthor();
author.GetDetail();
BookEditor editor = new BookEditor();
editor.GetDetail();
BookReviewer reviewer = new BookReviewer();
reviewer.GetDetail();
}
}
```

Above code-snippet contains only one public method that is responsible to display the operations. Display() method is one that gets the details of author , editor and reviewer of a book. At first glance, we can say that above code is with different classes of different implementation. But, actually we are abstracting our code with the help of abstract class, the child or derived classes then providing the details whatever the demand.

Consider following code:

```
public abstract class Team
{
public abstract void GetDetail();
}
```

We have an abstract class Team with an abstract method GetDetail() this is the method that is responsible to get the details of team. Now, think what this team include, this team build with Author, Editor and a Reviewer. So, we have following code-snippet:

```
public class BookAuthor : Team
{
public override void GetDetail() => Display();
private void Display()
{
WriteLine("Author detail");
Write("Enter Author Name:");
var name = ReadLine();
WriteLine($"Book author is: {name}");
}
}
```

BookAuthor class inherits Team and override the GetDetail() method. This method further call a private method Display() that is something user would not be aware. As user will call only GetDetail() method.

In similar way, we have BookEditor and BookReviewer classes:

```
public class BookEditor : Team
{
public override void GetDetail() => Display();
private void Display()
{
WriteLine("Editor detail");
Write("Enter Editor Name:");
var name = ReadLine();
WriteLine($"Book editor is: {name}");
}
}
public class BookReviewer : Team
{
public override void GetDetail() => Display();
private void Display()
{
WriteLine("Reviewer detail");
Write("Enter Reviewer Name:");
var name = ReadLine();
WriteLine($"Book reviewer is: {name}");
}
}
```

In the preceding code, classes will only reveal one method, that is, GetDetail() to provide the required details.

Following will be the output when this code will be called from the client:

```
Day 07: Learning C# in 7-days
Author detail
Enter Author Name:Gaurav Aroraa
Book author is: Gaurav Aroraa
Editor detail
Enter Editor Name:Vikas Tiwari
Book editor is: Vikas Tiwari
Reviewer detail
Enter Reviewer Name:Shivprasad Koirala
Book reviewer is: Shivprasad Koirala
```

Encapsulation

Encapsulation is a process where data is not directly accessible to user. When you want to restrict or hide the direct access to data from client or user, that activity or a process is known as encapsulation.

When we say information hiding that means hiding an information that doesn't require for user or user is not interested in the information for example - when you buy a bike you'd not be interested to know how it's engine works, how fuel supply exists internally, but you're interested about the mileage of bike and so on.

 Information hiding is not a data hiding but it is an implementation hiding in C# for more information refer: `http://blog.ploeh.dk/2012/11/27/ Encapsulationofproperties/`.

In C# when functions and data combined in a single unit (called class) and you cannot access the data directly is called encapsulation. In C# class, access modifiers are applied to members, properties to avoid the direct access of data to other cases or users.

In this section, we will discuss about encapsulation in detail.

What are access modifier in C#?

As discussed in previous section, encapsulation is a concept of hiding information from the outer world. In C#, we have access modifier or access specifiers that helps us to hide the information. These access modifiers help you to define the scope and visibility of a class member.

Following are the access modifiers:

- Public
- Private
- Protected
- Internal
- Protected internal

We have already gone through all the preceding access modifiers during day four. Please refer to section *Access modifier* and their accessibility to revise how these modifier works and help us to define the visibility.

Implementing encapsulation

In this section, we will implement encapsulation in C# 7.0. Think a scenario where we need to provide the information of an `Author` including recent published book. Consider following code-snippet:

```
internal class Writer
{
    private string _title;
    private string _isbn;
    private string _name;
    public void SetName(string fname, string lName)
    {
        if (string.IsNullOrEmpty(fname) ||
        string.IsNullOrWhiteSpace(lName))
        throw new ArgumentException("Name can not be
        blank.");
        _name = $"{fname} {lName}";
    }
    public void SetTitle(string title)
    {
        if (string.IsNullOrWhiteSpace(title))
        throw new ArgumentException("Book title can not be
        blank.");
        _title = title;
    }
    public void SetIsbn(string isbn)
    {
        if (!string.IsNullOrEmpty(isbn))
        {
            if (isbn.Length == 10 | isbn.Length == 13)
            {
                if (!ulong.TryParse(isbn, out _))
                throw new ArgumentException("The ISBN can
                consist of numeric characters only.");
            }
            else
        throw new ArgumentException("ISBN should be 10 or 13
        characters numeric string only.");
        }
     _isbn = isbn;
    }
    public override string ToString() => $"Author '{_name}'
    has authored a book '{_title}' with ISBN '{_isbn}'";
}
```

In the preceding code-snippet that is showing the implementation of encapsulation, we are hiding our fields that user would not want to know. As the main motto is to show the recent publication.

Following is the code for client, that need the information:

```
public class EncapsulationImplementation
{
    public void Display()
    {
        WriteLine("Encapsulation example");
        Writer writer = new Writer();
        Write("Enter First Name:");
        var fName = ReadLine();
        Write("Enter Last Name:");
        var lName = ReadLine();
        writer.SetName(fName,lName);
        Write("Book title:");
        writer.SetTitle(ReadLine());
        Write("Enter ISBN:");
        writer.SetIsbn(ReadLine());
        WriteLine("Complete details of book:");
        WriteLine(writer.ToString());
    }
}
```

The preceding code-snippet is to get the required information only. User would not be aware of how the information is fetching/retrieving from class.

```
Day 07: Learning C# in 7-days
Encapsulation example
Enter First Name:Gaurav
Enter Last Name:Aroraa
Book title:Learn C# in 7-days
Enter ISBN:9781787287044
Complete details of book:
Author 'Gaurav Aroraa' has authored a book 'Learn C# in 7-days' with ISBN '9781787287044'
```

The preceding image is showing the exact output, you will see after execution of previous code.

Polymorphism

In simple words, polymorphism means having many forms. In C#, we can express one interface with multiple functions as polymorphism. Polymorphism is taken from Greek-word that has meaning of *many-shapes*.

 All types in C# (including user-defined types) inherit from object hence every type in C# is polymorphic.

As we discussed polymorphism means many forms. These forms can be of functions where we implement function of same name having same parameters in different forms in derived classes. Also, polymorphism is having the capability to provide different implementation of methods that are implemented with same name.

In coming sections, we will discuss the various types of polymorphism including their implementation using C# 7.0.

Types of polymorphism

In C#, we have two types of polymorphism and these types are:

- **Compile-time polymorphism**

    Compile-time polymorphism is also famous as early binding or overloading or static binding. It determines at compile-time and meant for same function name with different parameters. Compile-time or early binding is further divided into two more types and these types are:

    - **Function Overloading**

        Function overloading as name is self-explanatory function is overloaded. When you declare function with same name but different parameters, it is called as function overloading. You can declare as many overloaded functions as you want.

Consider following code-snippet:

```
public class Math
{
    public int Add(int num1, int num2) =>    num1 +
num2;
    public double Add(double num1, double num2) => num1
+ num2;
}
```

The preceding code is a representation of overloading, Math class is having a method Add() with an overload the parameters of type double. These methods in meant to separate behaviour. Consider following code:

```
public class CompileTimePolymorphismImplementation
{
    public void Run()
    {
        Write("Enter first number:");
        var num1 = ReadLine();
        Write("Enter second number:");
        var num2 = ReadLine();
        Math math = new Math();
        var sum1 = math.Add(FloatToInt(num1),
        FloatToInt(num1));
        var sum2 = math.Add(ToFloat(num1),
ToFloat(num2));
        WriteLine("Using Addd(int num1, int num2)");
        WriteLine($"{FloatToInt(num1)} +
{FloatToInt(num2)}
        = {sum1}");
        WriteLine("Using Add(double num1, double num2)");
        WriteLine($"{ToFloat(num1)} + {ToFloat(num2)} =
        {sum2}");
    }
    private int FloatToInt(string num) =>
    (int)System.Math.Round(ToFloat(num), 0);
    private float ToFloat(string num) =
    float.Parse(num);
}
```

The preceding code snippet is using both the methods. Following is the output of the preceding implementation:

```
Day 07: Learning C# in 7-days
CompileTime Polymorphism Implementation Example

Enter first number:49.49
Enter second number:49.51
Using Addd(int num1, int num2)
49 + 50 = 98
Using Add(double num1, double num2)
49.49 + 49.51 = 99
Press any key to exit...
```

If you analyse previous result you will find the overloaded method that accepts double parameters provides accurate results that is, 99 because we supplied decimal values and it adds decimals. On the other had Add method with integer type parameter, apply round of to double and convert them into integer so, it displays the wrong result. However previous example is not related to correct calculations but this tells about the compile-time polymorphism using function overloading.

- **Operator Overloading**

Operator loading is a way to redefine the actual functionality of a particular operator.

This is important while you're working with user-defined complex types where direct use of in-built operators is impossible.

We have already discussed operator overloading in details during Chapter 2, *Day 02 – Getting Started with C#* section - *Operator Overloading* - refer to this section if you want to revise operator overloading.

- Run-time polimorphism

    Run-time polymorphism is also famous as late binding or overriding or dynamic binding. We can achieve run-time polymorphism by overriding methods in C#. The virtual or abstract methods can be overridden in derived classes.

    In C# abstract classes provide a way to implement run-time polymorphism where we override abstract methods in derived classes. The `virtual` keyword is also a way to override method in derive class. We discussed `virtual` keyword during Chapter 2, *Day 02 – Getting Started with C#* (refer if you want to revise it).

    Consider the following example:

    ```
    internal abstract class Team
    {
        public abstract string Detail();
    }
    internal class Author : Team
    {
        private readonly string _name;
        public Author(string name) => _name = name;
        public override string Detail()
        {
            WriteLine("Author Team:");
            return $"Member name: {_name}";
        }
    }
    ```

    The preceding code-snippet showing overriding with the implementation of abstract class in C#. Here abstract class `Team` is having an abstract method `Detail()` that is overridden.

    ```
    public class RunTimePolymorphismImplementation
    {
        public void Run()
        {
            Write("Enter name:");
            var name = ReadLine();
            Author author = new Author(name);
            WriteLine(author.Detail());
        }
    }
    ```

The preceding code-snippet is consuming `Author` class and produces the following output:

```
Day 07: Learning C# in 7-days
RunTime Polymorphism Implementation Example

Enter name:Gaurav Arora
Author Team:
Member name: Gaurav Arora
Press any key to exit...
```

The preceding image is showing output of a program example implementing of abstract class.

We can also implement run-time polymorphism using abstract class and virtual methods, consider following code-snippet:

```csharp
internal class Team
{
    protected string Name;
    public Team(string name)
    {
        Name = name;
    }
    public virtual string Detail() => Name;
}
internal class Author : Team
{
    public Author(string name) : base(name)
    {}
    public override string Detail() => Name;
}
internal class Editor : Team
{
    public Editor(string name) : base(name)
    {}
    public override string Detail() => Name;
}
internal class Client
{
    public void ShowDetail(Team team) =>
    WriteLine($"Member: {team.Detail()}");
}
```

In the preceding, code-snippet is an implementation example of run-time polymorphism where our client accepting object of type `Team` and perform the operation by knowing the type of a class at runtime.

```
Day 07: Learning C# in 7-days
RunTime Polymorphism Implementationusing Abstract Virtual

Enter author name:Gaurav Aroraa
Enter editor name:Vikas Tiwari

Authors detail:
Member: Gaurav Aroraa

Editors detail:
Member: Vikas Tiwari
Press any key to exit...
```

Our method `ShowDetail()` displays the member name of a particular type.

Implementing polymorphism

Let's implement polymorphism in a complete, consider the following code-snippet:

```
public class PolymorphismImplementation
{
    public void Build()
    {
        List<Team> teams = new List<Team> {new Author(), new
        Editor(), new Reviewer()};
        foreach (Team team in teams)
        team.BuildTeam();
    }
}
public class Team
{
    public string Name { get; private set; }
    public string Title { get; private set; }
    public virtual void BuildTeam()
    {
        Write("Name:");
        Name = ReadLine();
        Write("Title:");
        Title = ReadLine();
```

```
            WriteLine();
            WriteLine($"Name:{Name}\nTitle:{Title}");
            WriteLine();
    }
}
internal class Author : Team
{
    public override void BuildTeam()
    {
        WriteLine("Building Author Team");
        base.BuildTeam();
    }
}
internal class Editor : Team
{
    public override void BuildTeam()
    {
        WriteLine("Building Editor Team");
        base.BuildTeam();
    }
}
internal class Reviewer : Team
{
    public override void BuildTeam()
    {
        WriteLine("Building Reviewer Team");
        base.BuildTeam();
    }
}
```

The preceding code-snippet is a representation of polymorphism, that is building different teams. It produces the following output:

```
Day 07: Learning C# in 7-days
Polymorphism Implementation Example

Building Author Team
Name:Gaurav Aroraa
Title:Learn C# in 7-days

Name:Gaurav Aroraa
Title:Learn C# in 7-days

Building Editor Team
Name:Vikas Tiwari
Title:Learn C# in 7-days

Name:Vikas Tiwari
Title:Learn C# in 7-days

Building Reviewer Team
Name:Shivprasad Koirala
Title:Learn C# in 7-days

Name:Shivprasad Koirala
Title:Learn C# in 7-days

Press any key to exit.
```

The preceding image is showing results from a program that represents the implementation of polymorphism.

Hands on Exercise

Here are the unsolved questions from today's study:

1. What is OOP?
2. Why we should use OOP language over procedural language?
3. Define inheritance?
4. How many type of inheritance is available in general?
5. Why we can't implement multiple inheritance in C#?
6. How we can achieve multiple inheritance in C#.
7. Define inherited member visibility with the help of a short program.
8. Define hiding and elaborate with the help of a short program.
9. What is overriding?

10. When to use hiding and when to use overriding, elaborate with the help of a short program (hint: refer to - `https://docs.microsoft.com/en-us/dotnet/csharp/programming-guide/classes-and-structs/knowing-when-to-use-override-and-new-keywords`)

11. What is implicit inheritance?

12. What is the difference between abstract class and interface?

13. What is encapsulation, elaborate it with the help of a short program.

14. Define access modifiers or access specifiers that are helpful in encapsulation.

15. What is abstraction? Elaborate it with a real-world example.

16. What is the difference between encapsulation and abstraction with the help of a real-world example. (hint: `https://stackoverflow.com/questions/16014290/simple-way-to-understand-encapsulation-and-abstraction`)

17. When to use abstract class and interface elaborate with the help of short program. (hint: `https://dzone.com/articles/when-to-use-abstract-class-and-intreface`)

18. What is the difference between abstract and virtual functions? (hint: `https://stackoverflow.com/questions/391483/what-is-the-difference-between-an-abstract-function-and-a-virtual-function`)

19. Define polymorphism in C#?

20. How many types of polymorphism, implement using a short program using C# 7.0?

21. Define late binding and early binding with the use of real world example.

22. Prove this with the help of a program - In C# every type is a polymorphic.

23. What is the difference between overloading and overriding?

Revisiting Day 7

Finally, we are at the stage where we conclude the final day that is, day seven of our 7-days learning series. Today, we have gone through concepts of OOP paradigm where we started with object relationship and get an overview of association, aggregation and composition and then we discussed structural and procedural language. We discussed all four features that is, encapsulation, abstraction, inheritance, and polymorphism of OOP. We also implemented OOP concepts using C# 7.0.

Tomorrow, on day eight we will be starting a real-world application that will help us to revise all our concepts till today. If you want to revise now, please go ahead and take a look in previous day's learning.

What next?

Today we concluded our 7th days of 7-days learning series. During this journey, we have started with very basic and then gradually adapted the advanced terms but this is just a beginning there are more to grab. I tried to combine almost all things here for next step, I suggest you should learn these:

1. Multi- threading
2. Constructor chaining
3. Indexers
4. Extension methods
5. Advanced regular expression
6. Advanced unsafe code implementation
7. Advanced concepts of garbage collection

For more advance topics, please refer to following:

1. C# 7.0 and .NET Core Cookbook (`https://www.packtpub.com/application-development/c-7-and-net-core-cookbook`)
2. `http://questpond.over-blog.com/`
3. Functional C# (`https://www.packtpub.com/application-development/functional-c`)
4. Multithreading with C# Cookbook - Second Edition (`https://www.packtpub.com/application-development/multithreading-c-cookbook-second-edition`)

8

Day 08 - Test Your Skills – Build a Real-World Application

On the seventh day, we went through the OOP concepts in C# 7.0. With the understanding of OOP concepts, our journey of this learning series needs a hands-on, practical, and real-world application, and this is the reason we are here. Today is our revision day of the seven-day learning series. In the past seven days, we learned a lot of stuff, including the following:

- .NET Framework and .NET Core
- Basic C# concepts, including statements, loops, classes, structures, and so on
- Advanced C# concepts, including delegates, generics, collections, file handling, attributes, and so on
- The new features of C# 7.0 and C# 7.1

In the last seven days, we covered the aforementioned topics in detail, with the help of code snippets, and we discussed the code in detail. We started with the very basic concepts on Day 1, covered the intermediate stuff on Day 2 and Day 3, and then gradually went through advanced topics with code explanations.

Today, we will revisit everything and build a real-world application in C# 7.0. Here are the steps we will follow to complete the application:

1. Discussing the requirements of our application.
2. Why are we developing this application?
3. Getting started with application development:
    - Prerequisites
    - The database design
    - Discussing the basic architecture

Why are we developing this application?

Our application will be based on India's GST taxation system (http://www.gstn.org/). In India, this system has been recently announced and there is a heavy demand in the industry to adopt it as soon as possible. This is the right time to create a real-world application that gives us a practical experience.

Discussing the requirements of our application:

In this section, we will discuss our application and lay it out. First of all, let's decide a name for our application; let's call it *FlixOneInvoicing*—a system that generates invoices. As discussed in the previous section, today's industry needs a system that can fulfill its demand to entertain all the parts of GST that we are demonstrating with the help of our example of GST-based application to . Here are the main requirements of the system:

- The system should be company-specific, and the company should be configurable
- The company can have multiple addresses (registered and shipping addresses may be different)
- The company can be an individual or a registered entity
- The system should have client/customer features
- The system should support both service and goods industries
- The system should follow Indian GST rules
- The system should have a reports capability
- The system should have basic operations such as add, update, delete, and so on

The aforementioned high-level requirements give us an idea of the kind of system we are going to develop. In the coming sections, we will develop an application based on these requirements.

Getting started with application development

In the previous sections, we discussed why we are going to develop this application and why it is required, as per industry demands. We also discussed the basic system requirements, and we laid out the system theoretically so that when we start with the actual coding, we can follow all these rules/requirements. In this section, we will start the actual development.

Prerequisites

To start the development of this application, we need the following as prerequisites:

- Visual Studio 2017 update 3 or later
- SQL Server 2008 R2 or later
- C# 7.0 or later
- ASP.NET Core
- Entity Framework Core

The database design

To perform the database design, you should have a basic knowledge of the SQL Server and the core concepts of database. The following resources may be helpful if you want to learn database concepts:

- `https://www.codeproject.com/Articles/359654/important-database-designing-rules-which-I-fo`
- `https://www.packtpub.com/big-data-and-business-intelligence/sql-server-2016-developer-guide`
- `http://www.studytonight.com/dbms/database-normalization.php`

On the basis of the basic business requirements that we discussed in the previous section for laying our system out, let's design a complete database so that we can save the important application data.

Overview

We need to develop our database in such a way that it should work on the basis of *single system, multiple companies*. The *single system, multiple companies* feature will enable our system to work within a corporate structure, where the company has multiple branches with one head office and separate users to maintain the system for other branches.

In this section, we will discuss following database diagram:

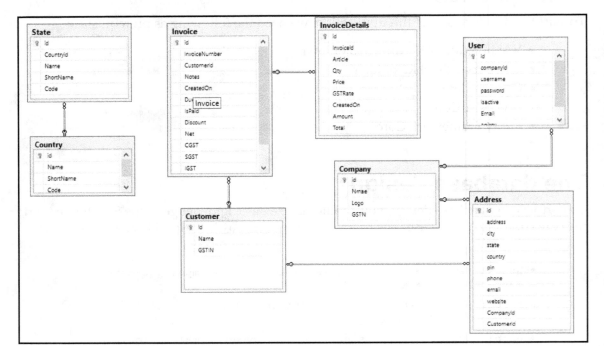

As per our requirements, our system is meant for multiple companies, which means that every company will have its own configuration, users, customers, and invoices. For example, if two different companies (*abc* and *xyz*) use the same system, then the users of *abc* can only access the information of *abc*.

The current system does not follow B2B or B2C categories.

Let's analyze the previous database diagram to understand the relational hierarchy in action. The **Company** table is referenced by the **User** table so that a user is specific to a company only. The **Address** table stands out of the **Company** and **Customer** tables, and is referenced by both the tables. Having the **Address** table refer to the **Company** and **Customer** tables allows us to have more than one address for each one of them.

The master data for countries and states is stored in the **Country** and **State** tables, respectively. The state can only belong to a specific country and, therefore, refers to the **Country** table accordingly.

 We arrange our tables in this way to achieve normalization. Refer to `http://searchsqlserver.techtarget.com/definition/normalization` in order to understand the concept of normalization in a database.

Discussing the schema and table:

In the previous section, we got an overview of our database design. Let's discuss the important tables and their usage in the system:

- **User**: This table contains all the data related to *users* across the companies. These are the users who can operate on the system. This table holds the user information; **companyid** is a foreign key with the **Company** table, and it provides a relation between the **User** and **Company** tables to instruct the system that a particular user is meant for a specific company:

Table: User

Column Name	Data Type	Allow Nulls
id	uniqueidentifier	☐
companyid	uniqueidentifier	☐
username	nvarchar(50)	☐
password	nvarchar(100)	☐
isactive	bit	☐
Email	nvarchar(150)	☐
apikey	nvarchar(50)	☑
		☐

- **Company**: This table contains all the information related to the company and stores the **name** and **GSTN** fields. The **GSTN** field is blank, if the company is not a registered company for GSTN. There is a foreign key relationship with the **Address** table, as one company may have multiple addresses. So, the the **Company** and **Address** tables exhibit a one-to-many relationship:

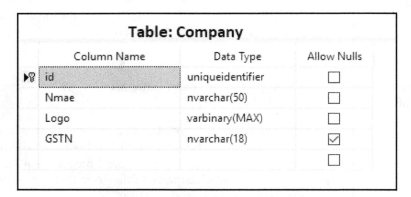

- **Customer**: This table contains all the information related to a customer, including **Name** and **GSTN**. The **GSTN** field is blank, as an individual would not be registered for **GSTN**. This table also has a relationship with the **Address** table:

Table: Customer

Column Name	Data Type	Allow Nulls
id	uniqueidentifier	☐
Name	nvarchar(50)	☐
GSTIN	nchar(18)	☑

- **Address**: This table contains all the information related to the company or customer addresses, which may be multiple:

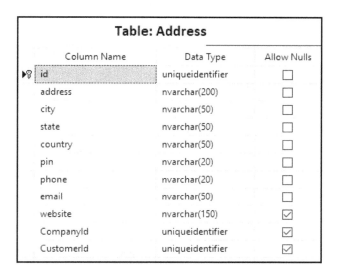

- **Invoice and InvoiceDetails**: These tables are transactional tables. The **Invoice** table contains all the details that are required to create an invoice, and the **InvoiceDetails** table contains the complete details of items/transactions for a specific invoice:

Table: Invoice				Table: InvoiceDetails		
Column Name	Data Type	Allow Nulls		Column Name	Data Type	Allow Nulls
id	uniqueidentifier	☐		id	uniqueidentifier	☐
InvoiceNumber	nvarchar(18)	☑		InvoiceId	uniqueidentifier	☐
CustomerId	uniqueidentifier	☐		Article	nvarchar(250)	☐
Notes	nvarchar(MAX)	☑		Qty	int	☐
CreatedOn	datetime	☐		Price	decimal(18, 0)	☐
DueDate	datetime	☑		GSTRate	decimal(18, 0)	☐
IsPaid	bit	☑		CreatedOn	datetime	☐
Discount	decimal(18, 0)	☑		Amount	decimal(18, 0)	☐
Net	decimal(18, 0)	☑		Total	decimal(18, 0)	☐
CGST	decimal(18, 0)	☑				
SGST	decimal(18, 0)	☑				
IGST	decimal(18, 0)	☑				
Total	decimal(18, 0)	☑				

- **Country and State**: These tables store the master record data. This data will not change, and no system transaction can affect the data stored in these two tables. As of now, these two tables contain the master data specific to India:

Table: Country				Table:State		
Column Name	**Data Type**	**Allow Nulls**		**Column Name**	**Data Type**	**Allow Nulls**
id	uniqueidentifier	☐		id	uniqueidentifier	☐
Name	nvarchar(50)	☐		Countryid	uniqueidentifier	☐
ShortName	nvarchar(3)	☐		Name	nvarchar(50)	☐
Code	nvarchar(5)	☐		ShortName	nvarchar(3)	☐
				Code	nvarchar(3)	☐

As per our initial requirements, the preceding tables are fine; we can add/update the tables as and when we get more or updated requirements. The system is meant for updates.

You can refer to `Database_FlixOneInvoice.sql` for the complete database schema and master data that is available on GitHub repository [<url>] in Day-08.

In the next section, we will discuss system architecture and the actual code that we are going to write.

Discussing the basic architecture

In this section, we will discuss the basic architecture of our application; we will not discuss design patterns and other architecture-related stuff, which are beyond the scope of this book.

To understand design patterns, refer to `https://www.questpond.com/ demo.html#designpattern`.

As mentioned in the prerequisites, our application will be based on ASP.NET Core, which consumes the RESTful API. This is just a basic version, so we are not going to show too much implementation of the design patterns. The following image gives a schematic overview of our Visual Studio solution. We have a presentation and domain, you can split these layers to more layers to define business workflow.

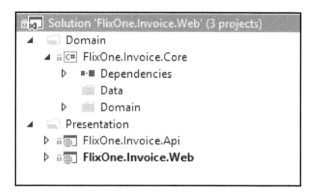

I wrote the actual code using C# 7.0; the application covers whatever we discussed on Day 7.

Complete application is shipped with this chapter on GitHub: <<Link>>

In this section, we will cover the main code snippets of whatever we learned up to Day 7. Download the complete application, open the solution in Visual Studio, and then visit the code. Relate the code with everything that you learned in this seven-day journey. For instance, see where we have used inheritance, encapsulation, and so on. Try to visualize the concepts we discussed in this book. You will be able to connect each and every statement of code written for our application.

Revisiting day 08

This is the revision day of our book. Of course, this is the last chapter of the book, but this is just the beginning for you to start exploring more C#-related stuff. On this day, we developed an application based on the Indian GST system. With the help of this application, we revisited all that you learned in this seven-day learning series, including attributes, reflections, C# 7.0 features, and so on.

Index

www.ingramcontent.com/pod-product-compliance
Lightning Source LLC
Chambersburg PA
CBHW080627060326
40690CB00021B/4836

9 781787 287044